No...... E934102   Class..... L96.67

Author ..... EDWARDS

Title..... Pleasant Abode

AVON COUNTY LIBRARY

PLEASE RETURN BOOK BY LAST DATE STAMPED

Pleasant Abode

A. C. Edwards

Somerset, that pleasant abode, which runneth to the Severn Sea.

Fuller

Buckland Publications Ltd.
125 High Holborn, London WC1V 6QA

ISBN 0 7212 0802 9

Printed and bound in Great Britain by
Buckland Press Ltd., Dover, Kent.

CONTENTS

ILLUSTRATIONS

FAMILY FOREWORD

This boyhood autobiography is intended to stop short on the eve of my fourteenth birthday. There are good grounds for this: there is, for instance, the well-known reply of the Kentucky centenarian when asked to account for his longevity. Moreover, most ordinary people rarely achieve anything in later life; their childhood is their only period likely to be of any significance to themselves and any interest to others – not, perhaps an unalloyed Age of Innocence, but at least a time to hold infinity in the palm of the hand.

As far as I know, nearly all the Edwards tribe from 1748 onwards and probably earlier have been farmers or butchers, or both; on the whole they have been better at butching than farming. In my branch of the family there are only five male exceptions: Charles, born in 1822, is said to have been a soldier; my father's cousin Joe was a draper; my cousin Hugo is a retired motor engineer; cousin Jack is a carpenter; and I was an usher who turned bureaucrat and then retired at the age of sixty-three years and four months in order to work really hard. Most of the Edwards' kinsmen by marriage also farmed or butched at least as long ago as my grandmother's great uncle, William York, a Bristol butcher whose working life stretched well back into the 18th century.

Nothing much will ever be known of the family history, for its members, though literate, were not literary and have left few written records. But do not think of them as dumb sons of toil: if tape recorders had been in use a century earlier they would have been copiously documented, for memory and tradition record that they have always talked incessantly: the only silent Edwards is a dead one. Where they came from I shall probably never discover; possibly from some miner who crossed the Bristol Channel to dig for calamine; but apart from being completely heterosexual, they do not display any Welsh characteristics. Wales is full of Edwardses, but of course they were the foreigners there, the conquerors, the men of Edward I. Anyhow, a chap whose mother's name was Binning can claim to be at least half Saxon. A true specimen of male Edwards is said to be blonde, beefy and florid and they still come that way from time to time, though since they married into the Yeates and other blackavised families, Mendel's law has had its effect.

As far as memory stretches back, they have been highly individualistic and independent, and this tends to limit the number of common family traits; but most of them seem to have been genial with slightly sardonic undertones. All of them, except myself (and, possibly, my middle nephew, Bill) have been firm Tories, and I detest most politicians. Generally, they have been somewhat indifferent to formal education, though I have never heard of one with a low I.Q. Occasionally they may exasperate their fellow creatures by their dogmatism or loquacity – or by their writings! As for a *dull* Edwards, that is a contradiction in terms.

9

Early on, they were moderately prosperous: the size of their farms and the house they maintained at Yarborough, Banwell, are evidence of this. It is also said that they were armigerous; if this were proved it would probably please some of the family womenfolk, but a male Edwards would hoot with ribald laughter, and then go and point the arms on his chamberpot. The family prosperity ceased a century ago with my grandfather, John Edwards, and his eldest brother, Joseph, though it had probably been running down ever since my great-grandfather left Banwell about 1835. My grandfather was cheerful, gregarious, athletic (he jumped his five-bar gates rather than open them), averse to hard work and fond of gambling. He frittered away two of the best farms in Nempnett Thrubwell and died fairly suddenly in 1881 at the early age of fifty-two, leaving his widow, Deborah and her youngest children, Aunt Fanny, aged thirteen, and Arthur, my father, aged eight, in great poverty for a short while. As far as I can tell, the four older children, themselves poor and trying to make their way, did their best for their mother and the two youngest; but this sharp period of privation left its mark on my father. In later life, he lost a good deal of money through mischance, misjudgment and generosity, but he never *wasted* any. Forty to fifty years ago he would often prophesy that I would eventually come to learn the value of money in the bitter way; now, at last, I am beginning to realise this, but it is too late for tears, and regrets are futile, anyhow.

For years my father's school satchel lay in a boxroom in my old home, and I still have one of his exercise books. It shows that he was a boy of considerable promise, potentially of university standard; but there were no Equal Opportunities and Welfare State in the 1880s. He left school at the age of twelve and was apprenticed to a firm of auctioneers; then, when his brother, Edward, set up on his own as a butcher and small farmer in the village of Yatton, he came to work for him and took over the full support of his mother. Uncle Ted did well and retired early, in 1904, though he soon lost his money (see Chapter fifteen). My father succeeded him, and, as his mother had died earlier that year, he was able to end a seven-year courtship and marry my mother, Emily Jane Binning, on September 19th. The Binnings were fair and Saxon until grandfather Charles Binning married Harriet Beakes, a lovely dusky beauty. Since then, the brunette strain has dominated, though my mother was so fair as a girl that she was known as Emmie Whitehead. I was born on 31st August in the following year, 1905. My parents thought there would not be any more children, but they were happily mistaken: my sister, Kathleen, was born on 11th February, 1913. I have no children, but the Edwards clan will endure: my sister married my cousin, Arthur Edwards; they have three sons and, so far, one grandson and one grand-daughter. I manage, usually twice a year, to visit them. The telly has a somewhat inhibiting effect, but when the damned thing is turned off, the Edwards family, I am delighted to say, are still capable of talking as much as ever they did in the past.

Chelmsford, July, 1969.

Postscript, January 1991

There have been many changes since 1969. My sister and brother-in-law have died, as well as a number of friends. My eldest nephew has sold the business, but he still owns the house, garden, yard and most of the outbuildings. However, the text of the autobiography has been kept intact. Chapter Eleven, *War in the Village*, was published in slightly abbreviated form in *Yatton Yesterday* (Vol. 3, 1986), the annual Transactions of the Yatton Local History Society.

Chapter One

THE LITTLE WINDOW

The little window was one of two, both narrow and fairly tall casements; but through the nearer one the sun did come peeping in at morn to strike across the bed where my sister and I were born. I miss that bed; my sister had it chopped up and burnt in 1955 because its frame was worm–riddled. It was no Bed of Ware and I have known bigger and better beds, but it was a solid Victorian beauty in deep red mahogany. It was five feet wide and had a canopy hung with yellow pelmet and curtains decorated with little bobbles.

Nearly all my earliest memories belong to this bed. For years I was afraid to sleep alone, and it was only when my sister was soon to be born that I was induced to move to the room across the landing. My own bed was a bed-chair alongside the big bed. Bedchairs unaccountably went out of fashion many years ago, but I note that they are coming back again: they were infinitely more comfortable than many convertible beds I have slept in.

As I lay wakeful at nights I could just see, beyond the big bed looming above me, the pale night-light which diminished my worst fear. I was convinced that the cupboard under the stairs was inhabited at night by a group of black women. They would creep halfway up the stairs and whisper to me, trying to induce me to come down; and I knew that if I did they would pounce on me at the bottom and whisk me into the cupboard. I knew exactly what they were like: smallish negresses with broad smiles and tall, domed, knobbly foreheads just like the terra-cotta pineapples standing where normally stone urns would stand on the flanking walls of Pineapple Farm, Uncle Willy's home. There were no fears by day: in fact, I often used to open the cupboard door and wonder how they could possibly drag themselves and me past the jars of washing soda, the packets of candles and the mass of empty jam jars and bottles. Nor did they influence my colour prejudices – I don't care much for certain white and coloured races, but I do like negroes and I look upon piccaninnies as the most enchanting of children.

My other night-time fear was mosquitoes. Even today I cannot go to sleep if there is a mosquito buzzing around. I used to call out to my mother several times in an evening, but she wasn't much good at finding and swatting them. She would promise to send my father up as soon as he came home. I used to listen for the sound of Paddy's hooves; then, a few minutes later, I would hear Dad's steps on the stairs. He would enter with a candlestick in one hand and a rolled newspaper in the other, and I was happy again. He was the most thorough swatter of mosquitoes, flies and wasps I have ever known, and he hated mosquitoes as much

11

as I did. He was probably dead tired, but he would go round and round the room examining every nook and cranny, standing on a chair or even on the bed, and every so often there would be a slap, followed by "got him" or "missed him". But he wouldn't stop until he was satisfied. Then he would stoop over me and kiss me; and when I felt the tickle of his moustache and the sandpaper of his rough chin, I knew that sleep would soon envelop me.

Most mornings, when my parents had departed, I would climb into the big bed, bob up and down on the spring mattress, watch the reflections in the highly-polished bed knobs and look across at the big papier maché apple on the top of the American clock case. But the greatest joy was breakfast in bed on Sunday mornings. My father normally got up well before six on weekdays, but sometimes on Sundays my mother would bring up a big tray and my share would be transferred to a smaller tray. Never was bacon so crisp, never had eggs such deep orange yolks, never were chestnut-coloured sausages as fragrant as on those mornings. Each of us used to keep some bread back to the end: the game was to mop up every bit of bacon fat and egg to produce the cleaner plate. Then we swapped plates to examine the other's efforts and argued happily until we agreed on the winner. Even the tickling breadcrumbs in the bed didn't seem to matter.

The landing, large and lofty, was lit by a skylight which often gave trouble during thunderstorms. Its floor was covered with linoleum put down by old Mrs. Wyatt about 1880. The pattern was beginning to wear off in patches when I was a small boy, but its surface remained uncracked. By 1955, the backing was showing along the line of a few uneven floorboards; my sister then covered it all with drugget, but I believe it may be still there, underneath. Its longevity is not entirely due to its quality: for the first fifty years of its life it was polished with beeswax and turpentine. Modern polishes save time and may well be all they are claimed to be, but they don't smell as nice. If I were a millionaire (and millionaires nowadays are the only people with minions) I would command my serfs to use nothing but beeswax and turpentine on my floors.

Incidentally, if I were a millionaire, and an old-fashioned one at that, I would also endeavour to engage Miss Ertha Kitt to sing to me regularly.

Against the one stretch of landing wall which was doorless stood a large wardrobe. Although it was cleaned out regularly, I firmly believe it was never thoroughly sorted out during the first fifty years of my life. In it was the hat-box with my father's topper for weddings and funerals (mainly the latter – he loved a good funeral) and the tiny tin trunk with my mother's muff which I used to borrow when I played guardsmen. Oddly enough there were also the two folio volumes of Rapin's History of England, always kept on a top shelf and never read. When my sister and brother-in-law were about to take over the house a year after my father's death, my mother and I were turning out the wardrobe and came across my father's wedding trousers – pale lavender grey and narrower than any teddy boy's. My mother's refreshing candour and realism was one of her many endearing qualities. She seized on the trousers with delight: "There! I knew I had put them away safely! Poor dear, I thought he would NEVER get them off!'

In the first room across the landing I soon settled down without fuss in the early days of 1913. It was normally the spare room, and I don't think I was allowed to stay there for more than two years. It was about twelve or thirteen feet square, a good deal smaller than my parents' fascinating L-shaped room. In the

Emily Jane Binning, the author's mother, aged 18

1066-and-all-that sense it wasn't memorable; indeed it is only very slowly that its furnishings come to mind. The walls were hung with framed texts, either samplers executed by Grandmother Edwards or highly coloured printed ones powdered with gold and silver dust. Perhaps these contributed to my early and enduring repugnance to the trappings of holiness. They gave me the same feeling of nausea that I get from children's corners in churches plastered with Margaret Tarrantry, or some of the tawdry accretions imported from the Continent by the Oxford Movement. To me, the real High Churchmen were Laud and his companions.

The furniture of the spare room was a job lot in mahogany: the best bit was an early 19th century chest of drawers which is now in my own bedroom. In those pre-First War days I was just tall enough to be on eye-level with the collection of odds and ends which cluttered up its top. I was particularly drawn to my father's cigarette case, covered with leather on the outside and embroidered silk on the inside and still containing two or three cigarettes. He gave up smoking in 1893 and the cigarettes remained there until 1918. I claim to be the only boy in Britain whose first cigarette was twenty-five years old; it put me off clandestine smoking for nearly a week.

Next to the spare room was a good-sized single room which was a maid's room until 1914 when my cousin, now my brother-in-law, came to live with us. Next to my parent's room was the long, large lumber room with junk which went back well beyond my time. There was a discarded hip bath, a fine place to play in. The thing to do was to sit in it, stick one's legs up in the air, clasp them with one's arms and spin round and round; my mother often wondered why the seats of my trousers wore out so quickly. Here, too, was an old family cradle full of ancient magazines with pictures of promenading ladies who seemed to carry their top halves about a yard in front of their lower halves. A few years later, the room was turned out and decorated and became my bedroom. Nowadays, a bathroom has been carved out of it and the remaining two thirds became Robert's room until he married. I'm glad he had it; he is my eldest nephew and very like me in so many ways, poor chap! Incidentally, there was no bathroom in my childhood. My elders used to take a big galvanised iron bath into the privacy of their bedrooms. I was bathed in front of the sitting room fire, accompanied by my celluloid muscovy duck and green and pink frog.

Between the single room and the lumber room was Aunt Fanny's fantastic boudoir. She was my father's unmarried sister. The furniture was all white with lots of wriggly rococo bits stuck on it. The walls were covered with samplers and framed photographs – well over twenty on each wall, including a large one of her mother, Grandmother Deborah Edwards, and a daguerreotype of her grandmother, Sophia Yeates, a tough old girl who during her long widowhood and down to her death in 1872 was an efficient farmer.

The dominant feature of the room, however, was Aunt Fanny's double bedstead – japanned, tubular iron in triple parabolas top and bottom, with trimmings of lace, or was it crochet or muslin? I cannot remember. On it was a feather bed of great depth and downiness – it had been made and filled by Aunt Fanny herself. She was very fond of me: in fact she used to say that I really belonged to her on the grounds that in a moment of exasperation my mother once said, "You can have him". She understood how long and boring a Sunday afternoon could be to a small boy, who was supposed to be quiet while his elders slept off their Sunday dinner. Sometimes she would let me come up to her room and lie down beside her on this wonderfully luxurious bed. Then she would read extracts to me from The Sunday Companion. In case anyone should think that this was dull pabulum for a child, let me say that I enjoyed every second of those Sunday readings. Looking back, I suspect that she embroidered as she read, for she had a vivid imagination. Once, however, there was no need for embroidery: The Sunday Companion issued a fat supplement on the Titanic disaster and, over several Sundays, she read every word of it to me. When she reached the passage describing the climax of the disaster she stopped a moment, sang a verse from Nearer my God to Thee and we both wept copiously. The Sunday Companion and Aunt Fanny taught me the meaning of tragedy. It was also a spur to heroics: for weeks I used to re-enact the story in my play. I was always the Carpathia steaming to the rescue; I even used to beg chunks of ice from the fridge to test the truth that nine-tenths of an iceberg lurks below the surface of the water.

But it was under the bed that the greatest thrills lay. Here she kept her spare high-soled boots - she had a short leg as a result of a bungled operation in her childhood. In the dark, valance-enclosed recess these looked fearsome – like sinister elephants. But it was in a box under the bed that the most tingling terror rested. Years later, after her death, I found it lying about the house, alas in a mutilated condition, and wondered why it used to make my spine shiver. It was harmless enough, merely a copy of Hervey's Meditations Among the Tombs, and other essays, redolent with the pseudo-Roman consciousness of the classical 18th century. It is in front of me at this moment, nagging my conscience – I ought to have it repaired, for it is an heirloom. On its flyleaf, in fine copper-plate hand, is "Sophia Sprod, Her Book, 20th November, 1812". She was my great-grandmother, that tough old female farmer. The end-papers list the deaths of various members of the Sprod family, including Ann, Sophia's grandmother. She was, I believe, the mother-in-law of 'Great-uncle York'. My father told me that his mother could just remember him –a strong-minded Bristol butcher who made a fortune selling meat to feed the French prisoners during the Napoleonic Wars.

But getting on for sixty years ago, I didn't know about this tenuous link with a distant past – with a Bristol well before the Reform Bill riots, the Bristol Turner knew, when the Hotwells was fashionable, when merchants still lived over their offices in graceful houses, and watched the tall ships sail past their windows. All that Hervey's book could evoke for the small boy was terror. Dare I turn over another page? the next passage might be IT!

I have just had another look. Here is a sample from those dreaded pages 44-45:

"Here, the sweet and winning aspect, that wore perpetually an attractive smile, grins horribly a naked, ghastly skull. . . Instead of sumptuous tables and delicious treats, the poor voluptuary is himself a feast for fattened insects; the reptile riots in his flesh; the worm feeds sweetly on him."

Well, well – poor great grandmother! When she wrote her name in the book she was eighteen, not the time of life to be dwelling on mortality. But I don't suppose she did, overmuch; otherwise I wouldn't be here.

Chapter Two

DOWNSTAIRS

Seventeen stairs in three flights led down to the dark enclosed hall, roughly equivalent to the large landing above. At the bottom, on the left, was the door to the best room, known as the Front Sitting Room but furnished as a dining room, though we ate there only on some Sundays and on high occasions. Special conventions governed these meals. The big, oval, gilt cruet with six containers was used, not the everyday, square brass one with three bottles and a mustard pot. The best knives were taken out of their compartments in the long roll of red flannel. They looked nice but wouldn't cut well; this didn't affect me, as I had my own little knife, my own chased fork and spoon out of their velvet-lined case, and my own little silver, hook-on napkin holder. When we had tea in this room, my mother used either her Chinese tea-set or the pompous Coronation service; and special jam dishes and cake stands and the silly, silver cake knife, with the prickly bone handle, were always on show.

Most of the furnishings were horrid, but I used to think they were magnificent. They were, of course, what one would expect decent people to buy who were brought up in late Victorian times and married in 1904. The dining suite was in heavy blackened oak, with lions' heads as handles to drawers and cupboards. I have since discovered that it was a popular design around the turn of the century. The sideboard had a high back and plate glass mirrors. A lesser affair, a sort of buffet, had no mirror. There was a small table, presumably for dumping dishes on, though actually it held the family bible, covered with red silk, the family picture album, with padded morocco covers, gilt-edged pages and a brass clasp, and a papier-maché writing case, with polished and tinted mother-of-pearl on the lid. There was a set of matching chairs, including a carver; they all had red leather seats, secured with big, brass-headed brads. The dining table was odd-man-out, a good, honest, oval, clubfooted, mahogany, Georgian piece. It had belonged to great-grandmother Sophia Sprod, and may well have been bought when she married William Yeates about 1820. My hand touches it at this very moment; in fact, most of this book will have been written on it.

The white marble mantelpiece and the high, sturdy grate disappeared long ago. Thinking back, I am now fairly certain that they were original, placed there when that part of the house was built or rebuilt in the 1840s. The large, elaborate, late Victorian overmantel reached to the cornice; this and the shelf of the mantelpiece were cluttered with vases and small photographs. The brass fender and fire-irons were bright with regular polishing; the fire-irons were never used – when a fire was lit, poker tongs and shovel were brought from one of the other rooms. On one side of the fireplace was a copper punch-bowl, with a George III halfpenny soldered on its bottom; on the other side was my mother's copper kettle, given to her by her sister Kate who died in 1907. In front, on the linoleum-covered floor, lay a crinkly skin rug. Near the fireplace was a folding, reclining chair with a prop-up leg rest; it looked relaxing but in fact was hideously uncomfortable and obviously designed for a skeleton eight feet tall.

The sash window, with thin glazing bars, sidelights and panelled shutters, seemed just an ordinary window to a small boy. Now, I know it to be a good dating point for the front half of the house, probably nearer 1850 than 1840, allowing for the time-lag in fashion down in south-west England. Above it, lace curtains hung from a bamboo pole. In front stood a rustic plant-stand supporting a giant aspidistra, greatly admired by my mother and Aunt Fanny, who used to argue over its ownership when they were not amicably discussing the best sort of liquid diet to make it grow even more monstrous. Gracie Fields would have adored it.

The room had a moulded plaster cornice and a plain, moulded rosette in the middle of the ceiling. From the rosette, a most complicated gas fitment hung. It could be moved up and down on pulleys, but it wasn't very effective – we generally used an oil lamp.

The walls were covered with a lemon-coloured paper sprinkled with white flowers, and this, in turn, was plastered with pictures. There were four Landseer steel engravings in brown frames – *Dignity and Impudence*, *The Monarch of the Glen*, *The Rivals*, and a fourth one I cannot recall. There were also three large photographs. I wasn't much impressed by the photo of my mother's younger brother, Arthur Binning, who died before my time; he looked just like any other harmless, amiable young man. The other two fascinated me. My mother's father, Charles Binning, died in 1901. He was known as Young Charles to distinguish him from his father, Charles, who died in 1900 at the age of ninety-one. I wish I had known Old Charles: he used to tell my mother wonderful stories of his youth, including one of a double public hanging for hamstringing cattle. Later, I worked it out that this must have happened before Peel's reforms during Lord Liverpool's ministry. But I couldn't stand the sight of Young Charles Binning's face looking down at me from its frame. He had mutton chops and a puggy nose. Bella Binning used to call me 'Uncle Charles' because she said I was like him – ugh! She was bossy and, anyhow, she wasn't his niece, merely his second cousin. Moreover, I knew then that I had a nose, distinctive, ugly, but decidedly not puggy. Recently, a young, former colleague said that I looked like a decadent Roman emperor. Fair enough; but Roman emperors didn't have puggy noses.

The third portrait is fixed forever in my mind. The photographer had captured and imprisoned the personality of Grandmother Edwards: a thin old lady in a mob cap; backbone as straight as a ruler; firm chin and humorous mouth, and eyes which seemed to bore into people's souls, sort and classify their merits and demerits, and then finally dismiss them. She died about eighteen months before I was born, and I could never summon up courage to ask the essential question. Dad and Aunt Fanny, themselves strong personalities, obviously had looked on her as a goddess. It was no good asking my mother – she would never pass an adverse judgment. But I knew from that portrait that the old girl must have been a tartar and something of a tyrant. Years later, when I was about twenty, I came on old Lily Tutton dusting the portrait. Tuttie had been a 'daily' and was then a treasured retainer. I said, "What was she really like, Tuttie?" She looked up at the face and gave that loud gap-toothed chuckle which I always found attractive – "Ah, my boy, she were a sharp 'un, she were."

In the hall was that cupboard under the stairs full by day of empty bottles and jam jars, brown paper and washing soda, and populated at night by those nobbly-headed negresses. Above it was a cupboard for dry goods and the current supply of bread jam and eggs. On one long side of the hall was the elaborate cast-iron hatstand, and in the corner beside it were umbrellas and walking sticks, including the one I coveted most – Dad's ordinary, everyday walking stick of cherrywood, with its delicious smell. On the other side was the peephole window to the shop. Above it were more hat pegs; below it were usually a couple of crates of mineral waters, either Archer's or Brooke and Prudencio's. My mother once told me that before I was born she had an insatiable craving for pop. This must have been passed on: ordinary lemonade or any one of the yellow coloured mineral waters was bliss to me, but Cherry or Raspberry was utter bliss. We were always mislaying the gadget for pushing down the marble stopper in the bottles; my thumb wasn't strong enough to do the job, and I used to watch eagerly while one of the grown-ups did the popping. Then I would pour out the precious scarlet liquid and shove my nose into the glass, like a pompous old greedy guts savouring his brandy. Actually, I did it to feel the tingle of the rising CO_2 bubbles.

Beside the cast-iron hatstand was the door into the back sitting room under my parents' bedroom. It was really the living room, L-shaped, dark, cool, a little shabby and very satisfying. Nowadays it has been considerably changed, and not a single one of its original furnishings remain in it, though bits and pieces are preserved elsewhere; but it is still a likeable room, remote, peaceful and quiet – when the telly is not on! In my boyhood it had only one window, with deep, wide casements, almost a french window. It faced north-east on to a little courtyard and a rockery with ferns, flanked on one side by the wall of the house next door and on the other by the end wall of the large larder. There were the usual lace curtains of that period on their bamboo rod with brass knobs on its ends. These wouldn't be completely drawn, but no matter – in the evenings my father, moving with his usual neatness and precision, would exclude the terrors of the darkness outside by drawing the panelled shutters and bringing their iron bar over so that it went into its socket with a satisfying snap. This was a decisive ritual, the moment when day ended and night began. I used to think of Genesis One – 'and the evening and the morning were the first day'.

In the corner of the room, between window and fireplace, was the old, oak-cased, brass-dialled grandfather clock by Joseph Quarman of Templecloud; Georgian; about 1770, but I didn't know that then. For five bob Dad had rescued it from old Mrs. Tinkling, who was about to chop it up for firewood. Like its rescuer, it was asthmatic – it wheezed and groaned before every stroke. A few years ago my brother-in-law had it carefully repaired and restored, and now it calls out the hours in a clear, ringing voice.

In front of the clock, Aunt Fanny's armchair stood on one side of the fireplace. It was tall and well-padded, but never very comfortable. Good for playing in, however – when I was on my own I used to curl up in it, with my toys around me.

Sometimes, Aunt Fanny and I used to play Cocks and Hens. She would sit in it and cackle; I would sit on one arm and crow. Then we would produce from its recesses the clutch of eggs she had 'laid' – usually half a dozen wooden bricks.

The fireplace had an ordinary grate, surrounded by pretty tiles with fan-shapes on them. The dark green marble mantelpiece of c.1880 was crowded: my money-box and, later, my sister's, piles of letters and circulars, family photos of the 1880s and 1890s in imitation cutglass frames without edgings. I cannot recall them all; but there was Hartley Hardwick, my father's cousin. He was unquestionably a good, kind man, husband and father, but I regarded him with that suspicion I have always had for the godly. His old father, that stern patriarch, John Hardwick, held family prayers every morning. They lived in a fascinating old farmhouse at Puxton – I always enjoyed a day visit to it but dreaded a longer stay – how I detested that diurnal knee-drill! I've been allergic to religion as long as I can remember. Religion to me should be a personal affair; by all means have it if you want it, but any attempt to inflict it on others is a damned impertinence. Anyhow, far more attractive than those family photos were the four candlesticks on the mantelpiece. Two were of brass. I don't know what happened to them but looking back from present imperfect knowledge to past imperfect memory, I think they were 18th century. The other two were copper (perhaps, once silver gilt) and late Georgian. As a boy, I thought they were wonderful, and I see no reason to change my mind. When my mother died, I gave them to my brother-in-law as a memento of her – they had been very fond of one another.

Dad's low, comfortable armchair stood on the other side of the fireplace. It was well-used: in middle life he was plagued with asthma, though he grew out of it in old age. When it was at its worst he would often sleep all night in that chair in front of a gigantic fire. It was fascinating to watch the ritual. When it was bedtime for the rest of us, already roasted by the fire, he would get up, walk over to the grandfather clock and wind up its weights by the clanking chain. Then he would pick up hearthbrush and shovel, carefully tidy up the grate and rebuild the fire – two large logs, end on, with a large chunk of coal wedged between them. Then he would settle back, kick off his slippers and place his feet on the fender. I often marvelled at his socks hanging in a row on the linen line – all the soles were scorched brown.

In the corner behind his chair was a small, round, country Chippendale table, still I am glad to say, carefully preserved by my sister and brother-in-law. Above it hung an oil copy of Romney's *Lady Hamilton as a Bacchante*. Near it was the door to yet another cupboard under the stairs; it smelt of mouse and contained Grandma Edwards' china and glass, stored there after her death in 1904. On the other side of the cupboard door was a rosewood chiffonier. Its cupboards were jammed with junk, including piles of Weldon's fashion books with their brown paper patterns; its drawer contained table cloths and napery; on its top, sitting on wool mats, were ornaments, mainly things which could be used but never were – a chafing dish, for example, and a most improbable earthenware, japanned kettle, full of old receipted bills, which went back before my time, and black-edged mourning cards to long deceased relatives and friends.

At the dark end of the room, a sideboard flanked the wall facing the fireplace. It wasn't really a sideboard, though that's what we called it; it was the base of an old dresser in elm, with brass drophandles (one missing) on its three drawers.

There were piles of books at either end, mainly Sunday school prizes won by my parents. There were the biscuit tin and biscuit barrel (Huntley and Palmer's Osborne, Petit Beurre or Butter fingers), the crumb tray and brush, a trio of cut-glass decanters (port, sherry and – wait for it – Wincarnis!) and three or four framed photos, all on wool mats. There was my mother's Singer sewing-machine, always carefully tended and maintained. Above the centre of the sideboard was a small bracket-shelf, with tiny photos in silver and purple velvet frames; and, higher still, a large oil painting of a moonlit scene – trees, ruins and a stream. Years later, I came across it in a cupboard; it was a poor, pathetic daub. In my boyhood, however, I thought it was mysterious and romantic. "Is it valuable, Dad?" He became elaborately solemn – "That picture, my boy, is worth a thousand pounds, more or less". I was innocent and gullible: a thousand pounds, coo! I hadn't realised the implication of the 'more or less'.

Between the end wall and the window was a long, hardish sofa, on which I used to lie when I had raging toothache. There was a cushion and a cylindrical horsehair bolster at either end. It was a good place for anyone feeling off-colour – its discomfort was so nagging that one tended to forget the other pain! Above it was another daub in oils, showing disconsolate cows paddling in a pool. Later, this was replaced by a framed sheet of brightly coloured scrap-book cut-outs of the Kings and Queens of England, from William I to Victoria, plus their dates and most of their regalia. Obviously a good thing – I knew my dates of reigns from an early age.

The dining table was good, solid mahogany. There were usually six of us, but it would seat nine in reasonable comfort. At the head, with his back to the fireplace, my father carved with great skill and precision. His lovely little Windsor chair had thin arms and spindles – Georgian, delicate in appearance, firm and strong in fact. On his left was, first, my sister, and then Aunt Fanny and my mother. I sat on his right, and next to me was my cousin, now my brother-in-law. Above Dad's end of the table, the gas fitment hung. I never did like the harshness of gaslight; not to be compared with the soft glow of an oil lamp. I suppose it was something to have a village gasworks early in this century, but, though Mr. Smith, the engineer, and 'Candle' his son worked hard, the quality of gas wasn't good. Our mantle would splutter and make raspberries; twice, at least, it overheated: the bowl cracked and the glass fragments landed just to the left of my father.

This Sword of Damocles worried us more than the Bottomless Pit: whenever we ate we sat suspended over a void – immediately below the table was a large, covered-in well, disused ever since the village had piped water, just before the limit of my memory. A few years ago, my brother-in-law had it uncovered and then filled in. He said it was beautifully constructed, in perfect condition and deeper than they could plumb at the time. He has been regretting this filling-in, but it is long odds against any mishap. It has misbehaved only once in my memory. There was a Sunday afternoon cloud-burst. A torrent rushed down the garden path and into the house. Dad organised us into a chain gang with mops and brooms to help it out of the side door into the yard, but the well complicated matters by overflowing into the drains, and they rose nauseatingly. It was a smelly Sunday evening, and we were too busy to be hallowed by Evensong. Attar of drains is not my favourite perfume.

The kitchen was large and dark, lit by one small window and three indirect lights. Its main fitting was a large, built-in dresser, by far the untidiest and most crowded dresser I have ever seen. The top shelf and part of the next one were crammed with jars of jams and pickles and anything up to half a dozen Christmas puddings in large basins. The household pickle consumption was prodigious; Aunt Fanny, chief pickler, found it hard to supply the demand. She would pickle anything pickleable: the usual walnuts, onions, red cabbage, broccoli and cucumbers, and bottles and bottles of apple chutney and tomato sauce. But she would also pickle marrow, runner beans, celery and even nasturtium seeds. Below the pickle pots were the usual inhabitants of dressers – cups and saucers, plates and dishes, glasses and wineglasses, jugs, teapots and coffee-pots. But the dresser was also a dumping ground for everything. Of course, a basin of new laid eggs, a jug of fresh milk, a basket of freshly-picked mushrooms were all fair enough, they would soon go (as we usually said) down the red lane. The real trouble came from those things infected with historical inertia. Take Dad's shaving mug, for instance. It was given to him by his mother when he first began to shave, but it had ceased to be used before I was born, as he had acquired a smart green and white one. There the old mug hung on a cuphook, year after year, and into it people would deposit pencil ends, odd screws and nails and keys which had long forgotten their locks. There was a pair of goffering irons hanging on another hook. Now, even allowing for the time-lag in the sleepy south-west, goffering went out when I was a baby. I saw Aunt Fanny use them just once; but there they stayed, a relic, like Darwin's Point or a bishop's gaiters. As for paper, it was everywhere, especially invoices. A coalman would deliver coal, the miller would deliver cattle cake: invoices – spike 'em on a cuphook! There they would remain, yellowing; and once a fortnight, regularly, a maid would solemnly clear the dresser, wash down the paint and solemnly put everything back again, including those revolting bits of paper.

The well-scrubbed, yellow deal table was large; it had to be-large enough to accommodate the hay harvesters (see Chapter 4). Beside it, against a side wall, was another piece of historical inertia, a mahogany bureau in slight disrepair, and never used, except for the storage of long-forgotten junk, never disturbed, except by myself, seeking odd scraps of velvet put there in the 1890s – I was keen on making kettleholders. It disappeared well over fifty years ago – I wonder where? Memory is tricky, but its shape and design are fairly clear in my mind: probably mid-18th century and worth quite a penny nowadays. A wooden bench, two Windsor chairs, three small 'kitchen' chairs and a coffer completed the furnishings. The coffer was used to store groceries. It was always one of my favourite pieces of furniture. I loved its smooth, solid lid and 'old-fashioned' lock. My instincts were right – I know nowadays that it is a nice simple piece of 17th century joinery, and I have it and treasure it.

The large kitchen range had a high mantelpiece with a row of tins on it – those attractive tins of around 1900, originally containing tea or biscuits and covered with oriental or rustic scenes. One tin was used for storing dried orange peel, considered to be an anti-fly deterrent if set alight and allowed to smoulder. Another was the button tin which gave me so much pleasure as a very small boy (see Chapter 6). A third was empty, and kept there by my mother as a memento and an object of affectionate hilarity. She baked a cake just before I was born and popped it in the tin. My birth caused a deal of trouble, and the cake was forgotten.

A couple of months later, my mother looked up and exclaimed, "Look at that!" The lid was a good three inches above the tin, thrust upwards by a fine quiff of white hair – the cake had sprouted a magnificent whiskery fungus.

Beyond the kitchen was a 'back kitchen', a draughty, lean-to, lit by a few glass pantiles. Here the scullery work and the weekly washing were performed. On one side of it was a coal store and boiler house with two large coppers. On the other side was the larder-cum-dairy, formerly a kitchen. I would rarely enter it as a child, simply because the sight, smell and taste of milk have always made me feel queasy. Here there was a plethora of it and its utensils – trays, pails, earthenware pans, skimmers, measures and jugs, all very ugh to me. I preferred the blue slate vat for salting bacon and beef – brine had a rare tang which made the back of the nose tingle.

Outside the back door was a long stone bench, really a flagstone-topped retaining wall to the lawn, which stood at a higher level. There, in dry, equable weather, the scouring of pots and pans would take place. I was never a scullion, but at times I was conscripted as knife boy and bootblack and plied my trades at this bench. How many people remember cleaning boots with blacking? a very long, laborious process, requiring much elbow grease, but the result was splendiferous. That old First War ditty must have been its swan song

> 'Charlie Chaplin,
> His boots are cracking,
> For want of blacking,
> And his baggy, baggy trousers
> They need mending,
> Before we send him
> To the Dardanelles.'

And how many people can still claim to have cleaned ordinary steel knives? We didn't have a knife machine, although, as a boy, I saw them being worked and wasn't much impressed. For me, it was the knifeboard, powdered bathbrick and a cork. I was a nice little boy who kept to the rules, but one of my acquaintances wasn't. He said that tap-water was no good for adding to bath brick, or, for a matter of that, to boot blacking. For both processes he preferred spit!

I find it impossible nowadays to see the outside of the house with the eye of a small boy. All I can recall is my pride in its utter solidity. Today, it still looks solid, not handsome, perhaps a little rock-faced, but comfortable and reassuring. It is two, conjoined, parallel blocks, with plain gable ends and a roof valley between which inevitably caused trouble from time to time. It is built of local carboniferous limestone, with some freestone dressings in the front; the only bricks used are for segmental windowheads and one stack at the rear. It looks all of a piece but just isn't: the front block is debased Regency building or rebuilding; half the back block is definitely *c.*1890, and the remainder may be of any age. One day I must sort this out, a suitable job for extreme old age, if any. I shall stay in Essex as long as I can do a decent day's work. Then I will go back home to await extinction with, I hope, fortitude and composure, and, perhaps, a certain amount of curiosity. But even in decline, one needs a little gentle form of occupation, and it might well be pleasant to chase up the documentary evidence and really know the building history of the house where I was born.

Chapter Three

THE YARD

The yard beside the house was my playground as a small child – my main playground, though there were also the garden, the two orchards and, when I was older, the fields beyond. The trouble was that I was alleged to be delicate and must be kept from going out and mixing with other children in case I 'picked up something', though selected children were allowed to come in and play with me. Sometimes I wondered if my parents were more afraid I should 'pick up' bad words than scarlet fever.

Anyhow, the yard remained my playground and prison. It was a delectable prison, large, long and interesting. At the bottom end were the huge, heavy double doors and the stone wall, shaded by a large sycamore, flanking the village street. The level of the yard was higher than the street, but, even so, the wall on the yard side was too high for a small boy to look over. Fortunately, there were several wide mortarless cracks in it for toe-holds, so that if I were playing at the top end of the yard I could run for all I was worth at the rare sound of mechanised transport, scramble up the wall by the aid of the toe-holds and watch Dr. Johnson's steam car go by, followed by a cloud of dust and a trail of steam and water. It really was a steam *carriage,* a steam-propelled dogcart, with the driver sitting higher – one cushion up – than the passenger. There was no bonnet: only a dashboard between them and a sheer drop of three or four feet. Sheppard, the chauffeur, steered with a kind of bath-chair tiller, and the great brake-handle, like an outsize garden syringe, could be drawn back with a grating sound along a row of ferocious iron teeth. Dr. Johnson sat on the lower perch, with arms folded, his spectacles twinkling in the sun and his little bag on his knees. Ten miles an hour meant an ordinary round; a reckless twenty meant imminent birth or death.

The yard itself was always full of life. In my very young days only my mother kept poultry. There was a very sleazy henhouse (later turned into a garage), fitted with rickety perches and orange box nests; but in the daytime the hens ranged everywhere. Those were the days before science was applied to poultry keeping; but I cannot help feeling that those free, barbarian hens, those noble (if ancient) savages, laid better eggs than the social democrat hens of later years and far, far better eggs than those of the brave new battery world. They were an odd lot, though, with so-called Speckled Minorcas dominant and a few Bramahs surviving from an earlier age, with puffy bloomers on their legs and little wings on their feet, like tired Elizabethan mercuries. There were plenty of

23

ducks, too, but only in the mornings and at night. Shortly after their morning meal was pretty well digested, they would hold an informal moot with a fair amount of quacking. Then they would form into a long file and be off, each wriggling in turn under the top gate of the yard; then, down the smaller orchard, across the narrow leg of Gammer's Butts, across the wide expanse of Hengstone, across the next two or three boggy fields, full of snakepipe, to the wide rhyne beyond. Then, at nightfall, hungry and quacking, the file would return to demand a good supper. They would have nothing to do with foreigners – the pair of Muscovies or the partially tamed wild duck. The hens, too, didn't like intruders – they harried the exquisite little Japanese Silkies, with black faces and soft shiny coats; they plucked at the phenomenal tail feathers of an unhappy Yokohama cockerel.

When I was a bit older, Aunt Fanny decided to keep hens. Steadily through the years, a line of henhouses and runs spread up one long side of the yard. She was scientific – she read poultry books, talked hens to anyone who would bear with her, went in for pure-bred strains, waged incessant war on rats which raided the bins containing the ingredients for varied and balanced diets; she even held regular conversations with the hens themselves. She was scathing about my mother's free foragers; but my mother wouldn't be drawn, though the slummy henhouse was refurbished and Rhode Islanders, Light Sussexes and other respectable creatures replaced the ancient crones.

Above all, Aunt Fanny, herself a great taker of patent medicines, would dose her caged denizens. She had a dread of constipation and gave her hens plenty of Epsom salts. These she bought a pound or so at a time, done up in blue bags, like sugar. One of these bags was lying about on the kitchen dresser near the ex-sweet jar which contained granulated sugar for current use. A maid thought it *was* sugar and tipped it into the jar. Her enormity was not discovered for some time, as bags of genuine sugar followed it. But one Sunday afternoon, my father took his first gulp at his cup of tea, served, as usual, in an enormous breakfast cup. "My dear", he said, "You haven't put any sugar in". My mother said, "Didn't I, Dad, I thought I had given you the usual four spoonfuls", and put in another four. Gradually, but too late, far too late, it dawned upon us sweet-toothed heavy tea drinkers that something *was* wrong with the tea. Nobody went to church that evening. We queued impatiently, but couldn't shift my father. Aunt Fanny, red in the face, was torn between amusement and dire necessity, but dared not laugh. My mother cried plaintively, "Hurry up, Father", but between muffled groans, all he could say was, "I can't, I can't"!

From time to time, various animals passed through the yard on the way to field, slaughterhouse or market, but the more permanent four-footed occupiers and guardians were the dogs, usually only one at a time, but sometimes two. Greatest of them all was Bob. He shouldn't really be in this story as he didn't belong to my childhood. But why should his long and glorious monarchy be forgotten and the dim and shadowy reigns of Tibber, Tiger and the others be recalled? It lasted from my later schooldays, through my university years and well into the 1930s. He was a sheep dog with a dash of lurcher; long and thin under the loins; brown, with a darker collar, a white and brown belly, white forepaws and an infinitely sad and highly intelligent face. He was a quiet and

Bob's harvest

most efficient worker, devoted to Tom Blackmore, his immediate master, gentle and friendly to all the rest of us. His kennel was at the top of the yard, but he was chained far less than any dog we had; there was little need – if he loped off to the fields for a little rabbit hunting, he would hear Tom's low whistle a quarter of a mile or more away and would come with the speed and grace of a West Indian cricketer at coverpoint.

Nobody deserves much merit for doing his own job well; and there is not much point in talking about the age-old companionship between dog and man – it has been done a million times. But Bob was something more: he was a specialist ratter, a rival of all top terriers. He would do a bit of odd, casual ratting on his own, but he had also a daily duty and an annual field day. It was the job of the first man to arrive in a morning to let Bob into the pigsty. This was a big stone building, with its entrance just outside the yard. A corridor ran down the middle; there were large sties on either side, but only two or three of them were ever used for pigs. One sty had a platform for weaning calves; mangolds were stored in another; in a third were the double hogsheads of cider; a fourth contained a large meal bin, a brick water tank and a brick tank of pig swill. Bob knew exactly what to do. When the outer door was unlocked, he would move silently along the corridor, snapping up any rat which crossed it; then he would leap into the meal bin for his daily average of two and a half rats, the size of the average English family (I've often looked for those poor little sawn-off point fives!). One day there was an unholy shemozzle in the bin and a dense white cloud filled the whole building. When Bob scrambled out slowly, he was blinded with flour, and stood patiently while Tom washed his eyes clear. Then Tom extracted and counted the corpses – there were twenty-two.

Every autumn, the adjoining sty was filled to the roof with mangolds. Rats will travel long distances for their food, if needs be, but they really like their living rooms close to the kitchen. The mangolds were ideal; they would hollow them out and make their nests in them. As the winter wore on and the mangolds steadily passed through the pulping and fingering machines standing in the corridor and thence to the cattle, so the rats would retreat deep into the remaining heap. The time would come when the rats would begin to go elsewhere if the heap were diminished any further; this was the signal for Bob's great day. The bolt holes would be stopped; several of us with sticks would stand outside the sty; Tom and Bob would go inside. Tom would pick the mangolds up two at a time and toss them into the corridor. Soon the rats would emerge, two or three at a time. This was chicken feed for Bob – a chance to get his eye in. Then the pace would quicken – they would come out in sixes, eights and tens. This was where real skill came in; no Time and Motion man could teach Bob anything; it was snap-shake-toss, snap-shake-toss. It was a poor hunt which didn't pass the fifty mark; the record was one hundred and forty-three, one hundred and thirty-seven to Bob and six to us with the sticks. Then Tom would lead an exhausted dog to the bottom of the yard. Bob would lie down panting, but able to wag his tail as we all stood around and praised him. Tom would kneel down and bathe his bleeding mouth tenderly, and any bites about his body. Dad would come out and talk to Bob like a French general about to confer a medal on a hero; then he would feed the warrior with sliced steak, waiting patiently (and he was rarely a patient man) while the sore-mouthed dog ate slowly. There was no undue sentiment: "That dog is worth a £100 a year to me for this day alone." It was a just reward, a special day's pay for a special day's work, the best for the best.

On the other side of the mangold compartment was the sty with all the double-hogshead cider casks. We made our own cider, or, rather, our apples went to Uncle Ted's or Uncle Willy's presses and they made it. I believe the average annual product was about two or three double hogsheads. One cask was always broached, and beside it was a two-handled pint mug with the Farmer's Toast printed on it–

Let the wealthy and great
Roll in splendour and state,
I envy them not, I declare it.
I have my own lambs,
My own chickens and hams.
I shear my own fleece and I wear it.
I have lawns, I have bowers,
I have gardens and flowers.
The lark is my morning alarmer.
So jolly boys, now
Here's God speed to the plough,
Long life and success to the farmer.

The cider was free at all times to our own men and to all callers, such as millers' men bringing meal or cattle cake. One day, a visitor forgot to close the outer door; the pigs from the smaller orchard came in, up-ended and smashed a cask and drank a good deal of the cider. As with human beings, the cider went to their legs: they were roaring cider-drunk; they grunted and belched happily; they struggled up and fell over on one side, got up, staggered and rolled over on the other side. It was a satire on human drunkenness, a rich text for the moralist – and very, very funny. My father didn't take that view; he was white with anger. It had been a full unbroached cask – one hundred and twenty gallons into the pigs or down the drain. He hated losing his money, especially if he himself didn't do the losing.

Right at the top of the yard, flanking the pigsty, was a stone cartshed; opposite the cartshed was the end of the stable block; joining them was a short stretch of wall, broken by the orchard gate. These formed three sides of a rough square; a temporary fourth side could be made by a long iron hurdle on wheels, thus forming a useful pen of, perhaps, three hundred square feet. Here sheep could be brought in and treated for maggots or footrot; the air would be filled with that strange composite odour of sheep droppings hoof parings and Stockholm tar. Here, too, with the cartshed doors thrown open and the shed cleared to make extra space, the sheep were sheared. I can just remember the whole operation being done with hand shears, but it wasn't long before we bought mechanical clippers and I was allowed to turn the handle of the wheel which worked them. I often wondered what the lambs thought when a shorn mother was restored to them, though there was clearly never any difficulty of recognition.

The tall, very solid, stone stable block was a special playground. Part of it was a coach-house where the gig and Jubilee car were kept, and along its rafters were nailed the prize cards won years before by Uncle Ted at horse shows. Sets of

27

harness lined the walls and the smell of leather and harness oil hung heavily in the air. Next, were the stables themselves, and, next again, an ox-stall, now a garage. Over the lot ran a large loft where I played on rainy days. It was a fine place for improvised skittles, for cricket or for practising with bows and arrows – bows of withy, bowstrings of picture cord, arrows of teasel stalks and barbs of elder. A great success was the telephone we rigged up, with one end by one of the loft windows and the other by my bedroom window some fifty yards away. The line was thin, silky twine; the receivers-*cum*-transmitters were empty cardboard spice containers with the metal bases removed and pigs bladder pasted over in their place. I don't know anything about the scientific principle involved – something to do with vibration, I suppose – but it *worked*.

Often, perhaps too often, I was left to play on my own. I had a reasonable number of toys, mostly German clockwork affairs, but, thank goodness, I wasn't given that stupid superabundance showered by overfond parents and aunts on so many children nowadays. I was driven to make bits and pieces for my own games, and these were much more satisfying. Most of them were indoor games and nothing to do with the yard. Perhaps my best outdoor success was in trains. Now, in my boyhood, two little boys who refrained from quarrelling long enough could play trains very happily: the yard was long enough for one to be a good, long-distance train, chuffing along with arms waving like pistons and mouth emitting steam noises and piercing whistles – always provided that the other little boy would take his turn to be the off-stage slave who would work the all-important signals. But a little boy on his own was handicapped. I spent hours making and fixing signals which could be operated by strings from either end of the yard just before I set off on outward or return journeys. I was never able to evolve an entirely satisfactory technique, but my signals eventually did work after a fashion, and I was happy.

Nowadays, I usually manage twice a year to spend a few days in my old home; and it still gives me deep delight – and sadness – to walk out into the yard and just look around. Aunt Fanny's hen runs disappeared long ago, though they had lingered on as coal sheds for many years after she died in 1929. There are no longer any free hens milling around; my mother gave up keeping them some five or six years before her death in 1958; and, oddly enough, it is when I am in the yard rather than in the house that I miss her most. I remember the times when she was in her sixties and I in my late thirties and I used to walk around with her as she fed the poultry: "See that nice cockerel? I'll send him to you in a few weeks time. That one over there will be just right for you about Christmas time". Otherwise, the yard had changed little. Some years ago, however, I found that my brother-in-law had had the whole surface covered in tarmac, a vast improvement. This recalled my most satisfying memory of it. It always used to be and still is a free parking place for friends and acquaintances – horses and traps galore on Flower Show day and other festive times in my boyhood; cars and lorries today. When I was about six or seven, the village street was being remade and my father allowed the roadmen to park their steam-roller, scarifier and other impedimenta there night after night. At that time, most of the yard surface was hard trodden earth, but about the fourth day Dad had his brilliant idea: he quickly bought loads of cracked stones from the local quarry; he held dark (and financial) consultations with the foreman and his roadmen; then, when road work finished for the day,

28

work began on resurfacing *our* yard. At the time, I was puffed out with pride the real, live steam-roller was making *our* yard, and I watched the nightly progress with rapture. Looking back, I wonder how Dad avoided a heavy fine or a jail sentence, but, as a former local government officer, who dearly loves saying rude things about bureaucracy and all its footling un-works, I must say that the whole business still gives me a very deep satisfaction.

Chapter Four

ROUND AND ABOUT

My father owned the house, shop, garden, yard, outbuildings and one orchard. Throughout my boyhood, he always rented the larger orchard, the Long Field and the two paddocks beyond it, and two fields, with a large garden between them, at the top of The Score. At various times he rented or owned a field beyond the two paddocks, another beyond the Long Field, one in the marshlands of Wemberham (locally pronounced "Wimrum"), another in the Wrington Road, Dr. Wood's meadows beyond The Score, two fields belonging to Cadbury House, a field in Claverham Moor and one or two bits of land in Claverham. Occasionally, he would buy the limited grazing rights in part of the wharflands at Kingston Seymour. These were reclaimed alluvium, still salty, within the sea-walls and right against the Bristol Channel. Its rich grass would turn skinny runts into sleek steers within a few weeks.

The garden behind the house is quite small, not much bigger than my 150-foot suburban patch. I used to like approaching it, not *via* the back door, but through the semi-french window of the back sitting room past the rockery with its ferns, up the little steps by the japonnica, past the border which held wallflowers in spring and my mother's favourite salvias in late summer, and then on to the lawn. Here, every summer, a large tent was erected and used for most meals. Have you ever eaten bacon, eggs and mushrooms out-of-doors at 7 a.m.? If not, you haven't really lived. At the far end, behind the Christmas Rose and the daffodil spikes and flanked by gooseberry bushes on one side and an evergreen and a lilac on the other, stood an ancient Quarrender, or Quarantine, as we called it, possibly the third best eating apple ever produced. When I was about five it became so barren and decayed that it was decapitated and its trunk used as the precarious end of a linen line. Then the miracle happened: it resprouted, and slowly through the years new wood and bark spread around the decayed trunk, new limbs stretched out and grew strong, and once again the tree became a prolific bearer. Down one long side of the lawn were three cordon apple trees and my own personal cherry tree. Against the other long side, the next-door wall, the jasmine, ivy and ferns flourished, and so did an incredibly ancient moss-rose. By the time this book is printed, my brother-in-law will have moved into his new bungalow, after a busy working life of over fifty-five years, too busy for gardening; but he has always found time to guard and cherish the moss-rose. I know nothing about rose propagation, but I will wager he will go to infinite trouble to bud from that old friend.

The rest of the garden was all fruit and vegetables in my childhood; its rich deep-red soil was always annually re-enriched – too much so once when some foolish person spread hen manure heavily on one patch, and we had pea-plants ten feet high and no peas for dinner. It grew all the vegetables we needed, apart from main crop potatoes, and these came from the large garden at The Score. The extensive rhubarb bed was memorable. Nobody ever did anything to it except pull the rhubarb and add more horse dung. As a result it resembled an ancient, deserted, semi-buried town, a rose-red city half as old as time. Red earthenware pots of all shapes and sizes (including ex-chimney pots), some partly broken, leaned at drunken angles. The rhubarb plants, pushing through the tops or out of jagged side holes, looked like the jungle engulfing Angor-Wat. It lay under a protecting north-east wall, and generations of dung ensured constant warmth. For a small boy it was a favourite winter spot; I would sit for hours on an upturned pot and enjoy the thin sunshine. The tortoise always disappeared into its fastnesses at the end of autumn, and in fine weather, old Fichu, the tabby-tortoiseshell cat would occasionally choose to have her litter there rather than in the back kitchen cupboard, where the boot-blacking was kept.

Best of all, I loved the garden walls. Nowadays their tops are levelled off, and they are kept well pointed. In my boyhood they were coursed in the normal way, with the rough-hewn limestone blocks laid horizontally, but the top course was jagged and set vertically. Some of these stones were fossil-bearing, others had lovely veins of felspar, many were mottled with green-gold lichen; and in the crumbling mortar of their interstices the wallflowers and valerian grew and flourished. Just below the tops were equally pretty parasites – the gold of the biting stonecrop and the pale violet clusters of creeping toadflax, or chookypigs, as we called them. Not good for the well-being of walls; but no matter: we are all parasites in one way or another, and a reasonable amount of live-and-let-live makes for happiness – and for easiness on the eye.

Three or four years ago, I took a photographic record of the smaller orchard. It has followed its larger neighbour and gone the way of many old orchards to form part of a housing estate. Don't rage about its fate: in this wasteful, expendable, never-mend-but-throw-away age it was no longer viable. Most of the apples were not worth the labour costs of harvesting; my brother-in-law told all and sundry that they could come and help themselves, but no one bothered. The price he got for that bit of land was more than my father left behind after a life of toil, but, even so, it is no more than just enough to ensure those little extra comforts for him and my sister in their retirement.

In the distant past, that orchard meant a great deal to me. Entering it was not easy – there was the strain of lifting off its hasp the dilapidated gate at the top of the yard. Then, past the main pigsty, the smaller one, the cowshed and the recumbent forms of sleeping pigs on the patch of rough ground. Past the heavy, hollowed-out stone pig-trough, where at dusk, a dozen or more rats in a row, would hang by their hindlegs, tails in air, to stretch down and feed on the remnants of pig-swill. Then would come the deep contentment of the orchard itself – escape into another world.

Dad didn't take that view; he was practical. He blamed Uncle Ted, the previous owner, for the state of the orchard, for not following a sensible policy of felling and replanting. His own fairly extensive replanting meant that for years there were too many trees short of maturity and too many which were really too old. But I liked this mixture of ancient and modern – I could see the annual growth of the young trees, I could enjoy the thick trunks and gnarled branches of the old 'uns, looking so everlasting. I was specially fond of the old Morgan Sweet trees. To Dad, Morgan Sweets were not marketable – shove 'em in with the cider apples and hope for the best. But it saddens me to think that there are millions of people who have never eaten a Morgan Sweet, in fact have never seen one or heard of it. There are two ways of tackling it. First, you wait until the apple is about a fortnight short of being ripe and its skin has just turned from green to pale yellow. Then you take it over to the wall between the orchard and Uncle Jack Crease's garden and bang the whole of its surface against a stone. This process is called by a word which is, perhaps, too rude for printing, even in this permissive age. Never mind, every old Somerset rustic over fifty-five will know it. The purpose of the banging is to release the juices. Then bite and chew. Don't swallow more of the apple than is unavoidable, otherwise stomach-ache will follow; spit it out, but let the delicious juice go down the gullet – it is like acidulated coconut juice. A fortnight later, the Morgan Sweets will be dead ripe, but most of them will be rather insipid, like a sleepy pear. Choose one which the wasps have got at – they know what's good.

Apart from a Tom Putt, the trees planted by Dad didn't interest me much; ancient varieties taste better, and what better than a Blenheim Orange? – you can keep your Cox's. And as for cooking apples, there is nothing to touch a Warner's King. We had three of these, all ancient. all still prolific and one of them bent over at an angle of 50°. Eaten as a steamed dumpling, of course. I was anti-cream as a boy, but the best informed opinion is that you should have both custard and cream with the dumpling, and masses of demerara sugar. Incidentally, demerara sugar isn't what it was; I'm told they produce it nowadays by spraying already refined white sugar with molasses. Not the same: better, nowadays, to use what we used to call 'moist' sugar, if you can get it – the fine, brown, sandy sort.

Nobody in his right senses eats cider apples, but we did have one cider apple tree which was an exception. I don't know its name, but it was like a small Pippin, rufous when ripe and rough-skinned, rather like that noble Essex apple, the Darcy Spice. Its flavour was like a Cox's, but more subtle. I used to save two or three dozen of these from the cider press and store them in my bedroom. They were at their best just about the time we broke up for the Christmas holidays. When I took those photos of the orchard a few years back, I picked and ate a couple, knowing that it would probably be for the last time. A melancholy act; but over recent years I've been getting used to doing many things for the last time. Never mind – old age has its comical side. Seymour Hicks said that you cross the threshold of old age when you first notice how young the policemen are. I would add that you've really had it, chum, when virtuous and highly attractive young women impulsively and warmly kiss you goodbye in the presence of their husbands.

Apart from the walnut tree with the smallest and sweetest nuts I've ever tasted, there was nothing else of note in the smaller orchard. The larger orchard was quite different; it had everything. I would enter it, not for a trip down the Lethe, but on an expedition of re-exploration, just to make sure that everything was still there; much as I do nowadays when I re-visit Salcombe in South Devon. It was really large, thoroughly old-fashioned; it was completely catholic – apples, pears, plums, damsons, several walnut trees, including one which produced double walnuts, cob bushes, masses of mistletoe and even a medlar tree. There was a romantic red door which led into the butt-end of the Long Field; there was an ancient pump which pumped water along a wooden V-channel into a tank for the benefit of the yearlings usually grazing there. Its most nostalgic inhabitants were a couple of russet apple trees and a Golden Rennet. How many people could put their hand on their heart and honestly declare that they have eaten russets? There is no flavour on earth which is anything like it. I know exactly what it is like, and I haven't tasted one for well over fifty years. The Golden Rennet is even more memorable, a peach transmuted into an apple. I am too lazy to look things up – this book is a holiday from the evidence-sifting toil of a minor local historian – but I would like some kind, well-informed soul to tell me all about the Golden Rennet; I've never seen a word about it in print.

The Long Field's real name was Gammer's Butts. Nobody knows who the old gammer was, but 'Butts' was appropriate: it was L-shaped, with a narrow, butt end, separated from a much larger square area by a stream with watercress, crossed over by a wholve. Through the butt end and along one side of the square ran a footpath which began where Well Lane meets the village street and really ended at Brockley Church two-and-a-half miles away, although, to be absolutely truthful, there was a four hundred yard stretch in the middle where it became a secondary road. It was a well-used footpath, peaceful and pleasant, though there was a short period when timid ladies shunned it and my father became unpopular. His cousin, Willy Edwards, used to breed prize shorthorns near Milverton at the other end of Somerset. Once, when foot-and-mouth was approaching West Somerset, cousin Willy hastily transferred his precious herd to us in North Somerset. When the scare died down, the herd returned, all except Bill, a ferocious-looking but thoroughly gentle steer. His home was the Long Field. When Dad and I took our Sunday evening stroll, Bill would steal up silently behind us and nuzzle the backs of our necks. He loved human beings. When he caught sight of a lady's bright summer frock, he would trot eagerly forward, and she would run shrieking from 'that wild bull of Mr. Edwards's"! "He would even come up twice a day to the milking shed at the top of the orchard and quietly take his place with the cows!

The Long Field and the two paddocks were separated from one another by marshland drainage ditches, known as 'rhynes' (pronounced 'reens') usually covered with duckweed. The upper paddock was high and dry, the proper place for a hay-and-straw storage shed, much frequented by courting couples. The lower paddock and the Long Field were liable to winter flooding. To mitigate this they were crossed by parallel rows of small ditches, or open land drains, known as 'gripes'. I liked these gripes. Ours were usually dry in summer, and full of cuckoo-flower blooms; the wet gripes in lower-lying fields were golden with kingcups every spring.

Sometimes the top paddock was put down to mangolds or oats, but generally, like the lower paddock and the Long Field and one or two of the outlying fields, it produced hay and was then used for grazing until the following spring. Haymaking was a serious, co-operative effort: never idyllic, never conducted by elegant young ladies in cart-wheel straw hats, gently toying with wooden rakes.

To the relief of all concerned, Dad, exacting and impatient, rarely took part – he was highly susceptible to hay-fever. Auxiliary labour was readily available, particularly from those who were on shift work and those who were drawing their 'Lloyd George', but were still able and active. George Warburton or Jim Wookey, the postmen, would say, "See you are cutting the top paddock, Arthur. About Thursday?" Old Tom Gurnett, the signalman, and other railway men would just turn up. They were amateurs, but they were also country men: they knew the drill, down to the smallest sartorial detail – take your coat, waistcoat, collar and tie off, but never, never have an open neck. Keep the stud firmly in position – hayseeds in the lower regions chafe abominably and impair efficiency. They knew their practical limitations – those who were good with horses would work the horse-rake or the waggon; the others seized rakes or hayforks and were content to turn, cock or pitch the hay. I didn't like pitching – it was a little disconcerting to raise a good dollop of hay on a fork towards the men on the growing stack and see a long grass-snake come slithering down from it. Only skilled men 'made' the stack – a badly-made haymow is a menace. Haymaking in hot weather is thirsty work, but most men knew how to drink wisely. Jars of cider in the shade of the hedge, were always available, but only the hardened drinkers took more than occasional swigs. Tea was best, and it was sometimes my job to deliver it; not an easy job to carry a yoke with two milk pails of tea a matter of five or six hundred yards. It wasn't so much the weight of the pails as the bigness of the yoke, designed for older, broader shoulders.

No pay was ever offered to auxiliary haymakers, or expected by them. Every evening there was supper provided in the kitchen. It was just as well that the long, yellow deal table was strongly made. There was a ham at one end and a great chunk of boiled silverside at the other. In the middle was an enormous 'truckle' of Cheddar cheese. Down the centre, from cheese to silverside and cheese to ham, were plates of bread, dishes of butter, jars of pickles and jugs of cider. It was a time of real, proper eating and drinking, much needed and well-deserved. I liked to watch my father carving away at one end, and somebody else, competent to carve (Aunt Fanny or one of the men), operating at the other end. Dinner plates were larger in those days – a modern dinner plate is about the size of what was then called a dessert plate. They needed to be large; they had to hold plenty of slices, real slices, not those pink, wafer-thin, almost translucent bits of tissue paper from the tinned ham on the grocer's slicing machine.

There was one other form of repayment. In the late autumn the same postmen and railwaymen would turn up unheralded, as they had for the haymaking, but this time they came with their wheelbarrows. No questions were asked – they just went round to the dunghill at the back of the piggeries and helped themselves. No wonder some of the railwaymen did well at the Flower Show – good, ripe, well-rotted dung was deeply prized and appreciated. I am no gardener, but ask any old, expert Adam: he will look back over the years and say, 'good, ripe dung – lovely! You can't get it nowadays.'

Chapter Five

BLOOD AND BAKED FAGGOTS

Men who pride themselves on being logical infuriate me; logical women are even more intolerable, but they are rarities, thank heavens. It is impossible to be utterly logical and still go on living. Take meat, for example. If I were completely logical about the horrors of the slaughterhouse which haunted my childhood memories, I would never touch a scrap of meat. If I were logical about my present-day revulsion to factory farming, battery farming, intensive farming, I wouldn't touch any of their products; as a matter of fact, I don't if I can help it, not on logical grounds but because I know my chicken, pig and egg will taste better if they have had a good run around beforehand. I like meat. I adore roast pig and venerate Charles Lamb; I curse my life-long and ever-growing dyspepsia which sometimes limits my consumption of bacon and eggs, that delectable dish, which by comparison, makes ambrosia, caviar, quails and manna, oysters and stout all taste like a dog's dinner. And what about those logical vegetarians, those 'rigid vegetarians', so rumbustiously codded by Chesterton? Do they ever think of those helpless ears of wheat ruthlessly cut down in the prime of life, those West African ground nuts being remorselessly crushed so that they may preserve their logicality?

Even now I cannot bring myself to write about the terrors of the slaughterhouse and my childhood aversion to handling lifeless, cold meat. Death, blood, evisceration and dismemberment used to send me out of the house or into my bedroom until it was all over; but it was almost impossible to escape the pervading smells which haunt the business of butchering. How far all this affected my childhood, I cannot determine. Memory is a tricky thing. As a very small boy, I think I accepted this side of my environment, maybe it was not until I was about nine or ten that I developed any kind of repugnance or near-terror, and made up my mind never to be a butcher. Incidentally, everything worked out very well. My cousin, Arthur, now my brother-in-law, desperately wanted to be a butcher from early childhood. He came to live with us, and soon it was taken as a matter of course that he would fill the place I had repudiated and follow my father. Arthur and I have always got on well together; nowadays, in old age, we both look forward eagerly too those all-to-short periods spent together exploring remote corners of the English and Welsh countryside. The trade which I could never have followed brings out in him that just pride, almost poetry, which is in every man, though stifled in many. He is that rarity nowadays, a superb butcher. He loathes factory methods, not on humanitarian grounds but because they debase

35

a golden currency. He can be lyrical over a prime piece of topside; his experienced nose can gauge the exact moment when chitterlings should be lovingly extracted from their boiling water. It so happened that, by the time he succeeded my father as senior partner, the farming side (that other occupation I had foresworn) had been allowed to diminish and virtually die – small-scale farming is not a viable proposition; moreover, the land is valuable for building, and, indeed, some of it has already been 'developed'. Sad, but profitable, especially as Arthur had bought the fields my father had rented.

There were some sides of the trade, however, which gave pleasure to a small boy. Butchers and their minions are usually cheerful and, when not engaged on the more grisly necessities of their calling, they are almost invariably very gentle men. They are among the world's most dedicated traditionalists, even in their politics: small tailors tend to be revolutionaries; farmers have been known to talk Tory and vote otherwise; but a non-Tory butcher is as rare as a tortoiseshell tomcat. As a small boy, I marvelled at some manifestations of their skill. Have you ever watched the assured speed of a good butcher whipping off a shoulder of mutton from a forequarter and the way he does it so that the maximum amount stays on the shoulder (the more expensive joint) and the minimum amount left on the neck?

Nowadays, many butchers work hard for long hours, but, fifty years ago hours were longer, largely I believe, because the tempo was slower, geared, as was life generally, to the pace and endurance of the horse. The predecessors of the present Edwards fleet of motor vans were a horse-drawn, four-wheeler van, a lightweight butcher's cart and a couple of bicycles with front carriers for deep wicker baskets. Only my father, and occasionally, Tom Avery, used the van, drawn by Paddy, a large roan. Percy Sheppard drove the lightweight cart, drawn by Kitty, the pony. A butcher's round took a long time. Somehow, this didn't matter; there seemed to be more time available in those days.

Sometimes, in the school holidays, I was allowed to accompany my father on some of his long rounds, all-day affairs, rather too long for a small boy. That is why I rarely went on the Claverham – Cleeve – Brockley round, where there was only one break, that large, cooked meal at the Old Inn, Cleeve, kept by the hospitable Cole family. This was my first pub and I tend to judge others by it and remain suspicious of anything plushy and pretentious. It was ancient, low-ceilinged, rather bare – a few tables, benches and chairs and settles on either side of a blazing fire; I am certain it would have looked much the same in 1812, probably in 1712. It was utterly clean, well-scrubbed, but no amount of soap, water and elbow grease could eradicate that acrid smell, compounded of yesterday's beer and tobacco smoke.

The Congresbury round was preferable. The break came earlier – about 2 p.m., a gargantuan cooked dinner with the Hancocks at Urchinwood Manor, an ancient house of almost mansion-like proportions. The Hancocks were a wonderful genial kindly couple. They had no children of their own and made a fuss of all young visitors. They had the knack of holding and cherishing their adult friends, and probably my father was their closest. Of course, as always in the countryside, the Old Relations Tie helped considerably. Mrs. Hancock's second cousin had married Uncle Willy, Dad's brother; George Hancock's mother had previously been married to an Edwards who was my grandfather's first cousin. Strangers to village life should never speak ill of one countryman to another, even if he knows that the two rustics are bitter enemies – they are sure to be related.

Anyhow, about an hour or so after leaving the Hancocks, Dad would say the magic words – "You can go off now. I'll pick you up about half-past eight." I would then run most of the six furlongs or so to Uncle Willy, Aunt Annie and my cousins at Pineapple Farm; the sooner I got there, the more time I would have in that lovely house. Cousin Fan, most warm-hearted of cousins, still lives there. Just to illustrate the Old Relations network – Fan, my father's brother's daughter, married Fred Griffin, my mother's sister's son. And they live happily in a house which I have always found utterly satisfying. It is nothing much to look at – a long, 17th century farmhouse with two back wings, it was given a face lift in Regency times, and was once a pub; but it has an air of serenity, its own ghost to titillate a small boy and nice, rustic, Regency fittings to delight that boy in his old age.

Although most of the horrors of slaughtering repelled me, I couldn't resist watching the early stages of the post-mortem ritual for pigs. I would draw near when the animals were dead and someone had removed the bucket of crimson blood, much prized for black puddings. Big baconers were laid out on the ground and covered with straw which was lit. The process didn't last long, but before all the hairs were singed off, the air would be redolent with that scent which assailed the nostrils of Bo-bo in old Cathay. Then they scrubbed and scraped the poor brutes. Porkers were scalded over a wooden tub and their hairs shaved off with a scraper. For a short while I was foolish enough to wonder if that was how layers-out treated human corpses! When these depilatory rites were concluded, I pushed off, not caring to witness the eviscerations.

Nowadays, slaughtering is done by anonymous persons in abattoirs, but when I go back to my old home, some of the old familiar smells are still around – cooking tripe and chitterlings, for example, and the roasting of breasts of mutton, all rolled up, like pairs of old-fashioned corsets. But I miss the penetrating smell of Aunt Fanny's celebrated baked faggots, eagerly sought by all gourmets in the neighbourhood. Not that I wish to consume faggots of that richness; even in my young days, when my stomach was stronger, they had a burping quality which would gladden the heart of any Bedouin host.

No, I would never have made a butcher, but I am grateful for being brought up among it. I know enough about meat to pity those men and women who go into my butcher's shop and say, 'Bit of mutton about sixteen bob' or 'Piece of beef about two quid.' Is it any wonder that factory farming flourishes when the country is full of ignorant clots incapable of choosing good food? I could no more slay a pig than fly, but I can choose a first rate, succulent piece of chump end of loin, and, in due course, do justice to it. But I still don't like the smell of any of it when uncooked. Not long ago, I was about to leave my old home to catch a train for Bristol, twelve miles away, when my eldest nephew said, "I'll drive you there. I have to deliver some stuff they urgently need at one of the restaurants." There the 'stuff' was in the back of the car – large, brown eggs from free range hens, prime T-bone steaks, a little pile of kidneys, aristocratic sausages (not half-bred), plump chickens beautifully trussed, trays of liver and sweetbreads. It was a perfect picture, a gastronome's poem, the very best. All the same, I was glad to get out of the car – I still don't like the pong of raw innards!

37

Chapter Six

FUN AND GAMES

Between 1949 and 1968 I met a wide range of people during the course of work – schoolchildren of all kinds and of all ages from nine to nineteen, training college and university students and a variety of adults from top-line professors to dotties full of original dim. I liked nearly all of them and made good friends, but I startled some of them and seriously worried a few by insisting that my greatest desire in life is to be left alone; and the desire is growing stronger every day. I long to be solitary and I am rarely lonely. I don't want aloneness for thinking, which at best is an essential indulgence and may well be a vanity; I need it to give a decent chance to that part of my being which lies outside mere intellect – I am certain it exists and I suspect it needs weeding, watering and manuring. Besides, aloneness is good practice for death, the one job to be done on one's own, the one buck which cannot be passed.

Alone, but not lonely, was the state I lived in during much of early childhood. Not lonely, because I had a good home and parents who loved me; alone, partly because I was an only child for seven and a half years but more because of that childhood illness which keeps popping up in this book. Probably coddling was essential between the ages of four and six, but my parents went on doing it for years when by the conventional standards of worldly wisdom they should have pitched me out more to rough it among children of my own age. Perhaps, unconsciously, they were wiser than they knew in committing me to aloneness for so much of my unorganised time – it makes kids find out things for themselves and invent their own play.

Oddly enough, my two or possibly three babyhood memories have nothing to do with play; I do not remember the incident of the Long Silence, an early instance of self-entertainment. My parents said they crept around the corner to see what was happening and found I had already gnawed away the top half of a pat of butter. Even now I adore the stuff, and frequently at the end of the main course I spear an additional new potato with my fork and gobble it with a similar-sized lump of butter – bad for the waistline and the arteries! Anyhow, I showed better taste than my sister in her Long Silence: she was found with her head over the scuttle busily chewing coal.

Parents, aunts and uncles, real and titular, and older cousins all kept me adequately supplied with toys. Not the plethora inflicted on so many modern children – I've seen them utterly bewitched and bewildered with about half the contents of Hamley's strewn around them. My earliest and best beloved was a plain non-curly Teddy Bear, surely the very earliest of those links with Roosevelt the First. It was cuddled so much that it literally wore out, and no amount of stitching could eventually prevent the sawdust from spilling. Next favourite was Dobbin, with his flowing mane, padded seat and little wheels on his four legs. Favourite No.3 was a pierrot with an angelic celluloid face. Noise was represented by a drum, a trumpet, two dulcimers, a tambourine and a succession of mouth-organs and penny whistles. There were clockwork toys, all made in Germany – an omnibus, a strong man who lifted weights and put them down again, another who played a perpetual game of bagatelle, a wriggling lizard and a beetle which moved in a slow circle, stopping every so often to make a horrid buzzing and flap his wings. There were also mice, but these worked by torsion, not clockwork. Some of these survived childhood and were stored in the boxroom, later my bedroom, until the mid-1920s when I handed them over to cousin Olive's children – all except the pierrot, and I found his moth-eaten remains in 1955.

Toys like these were all very well: I played for hours with them, but, apart from Teddy, Dobbin and Pierrot, they never gave real satisfaction A clockwork toy, for instance, is wound up and it goes until it stops, and that's that and nothing more. The imitative and learning toys were far better. The earliest go back beyond memory, the twenty-six bricks from which I learned my alphabet – 'C was a cat with its kittens at play; D was a dog whose name was Old Tray.' They were followed by a set of building bricks, which, according to the pretty picture on the cover of the box, would make up into the facade of a debased Greek temple. Quite early on I had my own little thimble and pair of round-headed scissors, and would cut out and stitch tiny shirts and pairs of shorts. When I was in my fiftieth year, my mother and I were having a good turn-out, following my father's death, and came across some of these tiny garments. She reminded me that I used to iron them when she was ironing my father's stiff-cuffed Sunday shirts – I had my own miniature flatiron, holder and stand. A little later I was given a toy set of a tram conductor's outfit, including a punch which would really punch tickets and ring a bell. This was followed by a toy set of carpenter's tools. These infuriated me; perhaps wisely they were made so that the chisel wouldn't cut and the saw wouldn't saw effectively. Today, I have strong views on this matter and regard the Do-it-Yourself movement as a healthy reaction to the laziness of this inept generation, slave-bound to the dubious virtue of time-saving, addicted to those devilish dictating machines, incapable of composing a letter and writing it in a decent fist and given to sending me a computer-spawned bank statement which tells me damn all. I am in favour of giving youngsters *real* tools at an early age, telling them how to use them and then leaving them alone. Perhaps this wouldn't work; there is so little salutary inhibiting and repressing nowadays that the tiny horrors would probably gouge one another's eyes out.

But I did have one real tool. When Charlie Durbin was building a brick swill-tank in our pigsty, he gave me a mason's trowel with its point so worn down that it was no longer of any use to a skilled craftsman. It was one of the best presents I have ever had. Charlie taught me how to make mortar, and for days on end, possibly weeks, I happily pointed the stone walls of our yard. Ten years or so later I happened to remember this and re-examined the walls; the pointing was still fairly sound and none of it more than about four feet or so up as far as a boy of seven or eight could reach.

Nowadays, in second childhood, I seem to have lost the capacity to enjoy one of my solitary boyhood pleasures – turning out. My home was never a tidy place, but when the debris became insufferably inconvenient, there were always plenty of cupboards and crannies into which it could be thrust. One of the drawers of the large kitchen dresser was mine and crammed with my bits and pieces, and provided I removed the drawer out of the fairway and into another room I was always encouraged to turn it out and tidy it up. Incidentally, this drawer was my childhood recollector; if I forgot anything I would open it, gaze at its contents, and usually the missing piece of information would be recalled. Forty odd years ago I mentioned this to Professor George Hare Leonard; he said his recollector was to smell his little harvest of japonica fruits. Sometimes my mother would let me turn out the other dresser drawers and occasionally, the cupboards below, crammed with boots and baskets, ancient and modern. Each drawer had a different smell. The end one to the right of mine smelt of Goddard's plate powder. It was a dustery paper-baggy, bits-of-stringy drawer, and down at the bottom was that lovely, soft high quality plate brush, which, in a more elevated household, would have been the butler's pride and joy. The drawer to the left of mine was spicy and full of dry goods. I would take the lid off every tin and jar and have a good sniff – nutmegs, sticks of cinnamon, cloves, chillies, prunes, rice, cocoa, cocoanibs and, above all, candied peel, possibly with some tangy sugar to be dug out from it. The far end drawer reeked of scorched oven cloths.

But the dresser drawers, the various cupboards, the wardrobe on the landing and the recesses of the large box room were all poor areas of exploration compared with that tall, square tin on the kitchen mantelpiece. My mother told me I would cry out to have it even before I learned to talk. It was the button tin, and some of its contents may well have gone back to the middle of last century. Rich Georgians wore gorgeous buttons, but it was not until Victorian times that ordinary people could afford extraordinary buttonry. The thing to do was to take my shoes off, sit on the middle of the sitting-room table, open the hinged lid of the tin and let the jewels cascade around me – common shirt and trouser buttons, wooden buttons, covered with Victorian fabrics, soft knotted leather buttons, smelling deliciously, large jet buttons of unusual shapes and cut into multiple facets like precious stones, and those small, incredibly fascinating metal buttons, looking like old gold and set with tiny specks of coloured glass.

When I was about seven, someone – I think it was Aunt Fanny – gave me a toy sweet shop with scales, weights, tiny paper bags and miniature bottles of real boiled sweets. This gave me great joy until the sweets all went sticky. Then, prompted by the vision of those large, bulbous bottles of brilliantly-coloured water in real pharmacies, I decided to set up a chemist's shop on the wide kitchen window sill. Keeping shop was simple: it was in a strategic position and I could usually induce the stream of passing adults to 'buy' something. The greatest fun, though, lay in making the pills and filling the bottles. Deep ingenuity was exercised in giving different colours to the bottles of water-plus; strange ingredients went into the pills and lozenges. All this continued for some time because my customers never *examined* their purchases; they amiably 'bought' them and then left them where I could recover and restore them to the shop. But one day, a more than perceptible hum began to pervade the atmosphere. My father had an enormous and active nose; I loved to hear him blow it – it was like Gabriel's trumpet, or do I mean Joshua's? He sniffed and cried, 'That blasted cat has brought in *another* rat.' Then he eyed my shop and began taking the corks out of the bottles. Phew! That was the end of the chemist's shop. After all, you can't expect bottled cabbage water to retain its pristine fragrance too long!

About this time, Meccano conferred its infinite benefits on the boys of Britain. I couldn't get near my set on Christmas Day, 1913 – or it may have been 1914: my father spent the whole afternoon slowly assembling a simple truck; all I was allowed to do was to hand the components to him. After that, I soon whipped through all the diagrams of models which my set was alleged to be capable of and started inventing my own. Mine, alas, was only a No. 1 set, and if I remember correctly those early Meccano sets ranged from No. 0 to No. 6; cousins Willy and Arthur were proud possessors of a No. 2. The Meccano people, with that sensible mixture of business acumen and genuine care for the customers' needs – a mixture so rare in this gimme-gimmicky age – sold supplementary sets, 1A, 2A and so on, by which one could build up to No. 6 by gentle assaults on parental pockets. But my parents wouldn't play: they were never lacking in love for me for the forty-nine and fifty-three years I had them, but to them Meccano was just a toy which a boy would grow out of and then be ready for something quite different. The trouble, perhaps the blessing, was their utter unawareness of the possibilities of education; they were not agin it – it just didn't enter their orbit, except perhaps as something which wealthy parents bought for their children. They didn't realise that Meccano was a pioneering educational tool. Perhaps they were right: I've grown weary of Education and many of its modern manifestations; who today could have much confidence in a man who said the grammar schools would be destroyed 'over my dead body'? Anyhow, my Meccano set gradually disappeared as the bits and pieces were used for home-made toys including a somewhat unsatisfactory periscope.

There was a shortage of books in my boyhood home; indeed, I didn't own a dictionary until I was thirteen. The Sunday School prizes of my father and mother were heavy didactic reading and may well have been one of the factors which have made me allergic to religion. How many people under seventy have ploughed through that sad, pious little book called, "Golden, Golden, All Golden"? Of course there was Rapin's History of England with its f-like esses. There was also a Victorian anthology which had lost its covers; it offered the more maudlin efforts of Wordsworth and a liberal sprinkling of Mrs. Hemans, Eliza Cook and the admirable Taylor sisters. A much better job was my own anthology, called, I believe, The Never Never Land – it is probably still buried in the impenetrable jungle of my boxroom a few yards away. It contained 'How Many Miles to Babylon?', 'I had a Little Nut Tree' and Stevenson's 'Land of Counterpane', several funny bits, 'The Lost Doll' and those verses about the old woman who went to market and fell asleep by the roadside. Aunt Fanny used to read it aloud, 'with expression', and the sobbing began when she came to the verse

'By came a peddler whose name was Stout.
He cut her petticoats all round about,
He cut her petticoats up to her knees,
Which made the old woman to shiver and freeze.'

41

She knew exactly how to strike delicious terror into the tear ducts of a small boy. Grimm's Fairy Tales, however, was a different kettle of piranhas; they penetrate to the depths of fear and should be banned to children.

The absence of books was not really serious. I was told later that I could read fluently at the age of four, but that illness around 1909-10 left its mark – at eight I was a poor stumbling reader. It was 'Uncle' Jack Crease who came to the rescue. He lived next door but one, and his garden flanked our smaller orchard. He was a great reader and a heavy smoker, and he was fond of me. I had all his cigarette cards and a book every Christmas, including those 'Wonder' books, so rightly named. Moreover, when I was about eleven, he and his son, John, gave me the run of their bookcases – there were bookcases everywhere, even on the landing of that friendly house. I used to wonder why it smelt so fragrantly; later, I knew – it smelt of books! I was then well away; soon other friends began to lend books to that little glutton for reading.

For my first ten or twelve years, my parents would not allow ordinary playing cards in the house – their fathers had both lost too much money that way! Later, they changed their minds, and Dad became an ardent whist player. Other games – happy families, ludo, halma, draughts, snakes and ladders, were always O.K.; so were wire puzzles and that peculiar panorama in a shallow, glass-topped box – you held it in both hands and, by adroit turning of the wrists, tried to steer a metal marble along a winding road from bottom to top and avoid the holes. If the marble went down a hole it would reappear at the bottom and you had to begin again. Somehow, it reminded me of Pilgrim's Progress.

But my favourite was my large box of dominoes – a Double-Nine set, much better than the standard Double-Six set. We played the ordinary game occasionally, but preferred Threes-or-Fives, my father with his copying pencil keeping the scores in little gates of five – four upright strokes and one across. There was no quarter for me, the child: apart from mother who couldn't count quickly and had none of the aggressive qualities of the Edwards tribe, the adults all played fiercely to win. If two or three rows of 'gates' reached the nineties together, the excitement was intense; but as soon as one of us reached one hundred, everyone relaxed happily and there were smiles all round.

When I was on my own, the dominoes were equally delectable: I played soldiers with them for hours. My side were the Nines, the Sixes, the Threes and Double-Blank; the enemy were the rest of them; the doubles were officers and, of course, my general was Double-Nine. I would stand the 'soldiers' up on their ends at either end of the sitting room table. The fact that I was outnumbered by thirty-three to twenty-two didn't worry young Clausewitz, though I took great care in the disposition of my forces, giving the maximum protection to my favourite soldier, Six-Three. I would go to my end of the table, place a pencil with about an inch jutting out beyond the edge, shut my eyes, give the pencil a sharp slap and send it hurtling towards the enemy. Then I would go to the other end, remove their dead and fire at my troops. The battle went on until one side was annihilated. If my army won, the survivors were awarded suitable imaginary decorations; if Six-Three survived, he had the Victoria Cross.

One of the solaces of increasing age is that one's boyhood was lived before the age of mass-media entertainment – or nearly so. The rollerskating craze came to our village and soon died, leaving behind an unwanted skating-rink at the far end of Rock Road. Then, for a short time in the winter of 1912-13, a travelling cinema put on a show there on Saturday evenings. My first film was a series of shots of the First Balkan War, strung loosely together. It put me firmly on the side of the Turks; I have been there ever since, and felt sad when Turkey came in on the other side in the First World War. Later on, I used to visit the cinema at Clevedon and follow the Exploits of Elaine. There was also a little cinema in the Arcade at Weston-Super-Mare. It was shaped like a bus, a 'driver' sat in front and the 'passengers' behind him, and the screen was – the screen! They showed films of Alpine drives, and when the view turned on a sharp mountain bend, the whole 'bus' lurched violently and we all screamed.

Otherwise, no mass media; my boyhood entertainment was like a real oil painting, all done by hand. We didn't go to the Bristol theatres until after the First War; my parents thought plays and actors were not quite respectable. Dad went to a pantomime – in 1897 or thereabouts; this supplied him with an adequate repertoire of songs until his second visit around 1921. However, there was always the annual Congresbury fair, with its roundabouts and swings, its water squirters, its fairings and sugar almonds, its naphtha or acetylene lights and those marvellous traction engines with their canopies held up by twisted barley sugar pillars of gleaming brass or copper. And there was always the annual circus in the field opposite Wake and Dean's factory at the other end of the village. I didn't care much for the wild animals, not because of their caged life (that was an adult reaction, and a strong one) but because they looked so scruffy – there were better specimens in Clifton Zoo. But the clowns were sheer heaven, a most fundamental form of acting, as Shakespeare knew so well. And the cornier the better. Do you remember the clown trotting on with his little wooden horse?

Clown: "Which island in the Aegean Sea is this?"
Stooge: "No, which island in the Aegean is it?"
Clown: "Why, Deal-'oss."
Clown goes off and comes trotting back again
Clown: "Now, which Aegean island is this?"
Stooge: "Which island is it?"
Clown: "Why, Same-'oss."

The pun has been with me ever since, and I must remember to work one into this book, probably right at the end. The best I ever made are not mentionable except in medical or heraldic company.

From time to time down the village street came the organ-grinder with his melancholy monkey in a red fez and jacket; the hurdy-gurdy men; German bands with real Ach-ing Germans; the man with the mechanical marionettes; and, literally above all, men on stilts wearing top hats (the men, I mean). Aunt Fanny and I would hurry upstairs and lean out of her bedroom window to put our pennies in the hat. There was also, *mirabile dictu,* a Lenten 'entertainment' held about 1911 (before we had our church hall) in the church itself – a real magic lantern show, once a week throughout Lent. It was Pilgrims Progress in coloured slides, every lecture stopping at a dramatic moment – would Christian get past those lions? Would Apollyon triumph? I longed for next Wednesday. It was better than waiting for the next instalment of Weary Willie and Tired Tim, or Ike and Mike, They're Both Alike!

One present, not a toy, ought to be mentioned because it gave me unbounded pride and joy. I have always abhorred milk, other than Bristol Milk. In 1913, my parents, worried by my thinness, said they would give me a silver watch if I would take bread-and-milk once a day for a year; Aunt Fanny promised a silver chain and Uncle Ted and Aunt Lily a watch stand. The watch, still working, is almost the only piece of mechanism which has never terrified me or let me down. I've never owned a car or rented a telephone; I haven't a telly; my other watches – except one – and even fountain pens go wrong on me. But is there anyone else in the world who has won a watch for eating bread-and-milk and kept it for going on for sixty years? Mind you, since 31st August, 1914, I have never looked a cow in the face.

Chapter Seven

CHURCH AND CHAPEL

In our village, as in thousands of others, you went to Chapel and supported Mr. Asquith or you went to Church and cursed his giblets; that crack about the Church of England being the Conservative party at prayer was *99%* true. The few village Roman Catholics went to mass at Clevedon. The wicked stayed at home or boozed in pubs, and when they died they went to hell and burned eternally. Life was simple in those days.

We were C. of E. and True Blue. This was the Edwards' tradition, though during that acute period of poverty in the 1880s they lapsed into Methodism for a decade or so. My mother's family were staunchly Anglican: how could anybody named Binning be otherwise? Their Saxon forebears probably disapproved of the Flight to Rome following the Synod of Whitby.

We were well supplied with tabernacles. There was a United Methodist chapel halfway down the village street and another in the hamlet of Claverham. The Brethren had a chapel at Horsecastle right at the bottom end of the village. The Friends, then very few in number, met occasionally in a room in the Undenominational School, itself of early 18th century Quaker origin, or less often in the Claverham Meeting House, a late 17th and 18th century building of considerable charm until its drastic restoration in recent years. At Claverham, too, was the Anglican mission church of St. Barnabas. Finally, there was the parish church of St. Mary the Virgin.

This magnificent church is always in my heart and often in my mind – I spend some time in it whenever I return home; and before it is seen with the eyes of childhood it deserves a brief glance from those eyes, now on the verge of old age. Large and cruciform, it is made of Dundry stone, silver grey with a faint flush of gold. It was built, or rather completely rebuilt during the ten or twenty years on either side of 1300. Then in the 15th century it was extensively but not completely remodelled in Perpendicular style – they left the flowing Decorated tracery in the south window of the south transept; and when this had to be renewed in 1906 the wise craftsmen went to the long disused quarries of Dundry and found just enough stone for the job. Inside, the nave, aisles, crossing and chancel suffered superficially in 1872, but even the Victorians at their worst would have been incapable of debasing the majesty of it all. The transepts and north chapel escaped, to be treated by more kindly hands in 1906. The church's fittings, as the Royal Commission investigators often say in their astringent, dead-pan way, 'are noteworthy': the alabaster head of Sir Richard Newton's effigy is

45

modelled with great sensitivity; the relief of the Annunciation on his son's monument has a simplicity which is endearing.

But I didn't begin to be ecclesiological until I was twelve or thirteen. Then it was fun to be put on to recording the inscriptions on 18th and early 19th century tombstones with their folk art carvings of *putti*, hourglasses and skulls and crossbones. It was better still to be drawing that fragment of carved stone on the side of the easternmost window of the north aisle, virtually all that was left of the splendid roodscreen destroyed at the Reformation. But best of all they showed me the mid 15th century churchwardens' accounts which tell the story of the screen's building – how the village sent a deputation to look at a screen in a church some miles away; how John Cross of Claverham, the local craftsman, like a temperamental *Prima donna*, had to be keep sweet–

'Item, 2$\frac{1}{2}$d in ale for John Cross to keep him well-willed while he works'.

Earlier still, I was fascinated by the truncated spire, the 'pepper pot', on the central tower. It was an architectural accident – the lofty tower just could not take a full stone spire – but I used to grow indignant when strangers found it odd; to me it gave the church that final touch of perfection. It is still perfect to me; and whenever I travel from Essex to my old home I stand up in my compartment as soon as the train passes Chelvey; I know that in a few seconds I shall have my first sight of that beloved pepper pot, three to four miles away.

The amount of churchgoing varied during my boyhood; it depended entirely on my father. When I was small we went fairly regularly to matins and evensong, possibly about three times per two Sundays. Occasionally, however, on summer Sunday evenings we would go for a walk across our fields and our neighbours' so that Dad could cast his expert eye along the backbones of cattle and the line and state of hedgerows; this was more enjoyable than church. Then, when I was about nine (or it may have been a year or so either way) my father and Aunt Fanny became devout. They were confirmed at Wells Cathedral – the earlier omission no doubt had been due to that Methodist era around 1880. Dad became a regular instead of an occasional sidesman, and eventually he was chosen to be Vicar's Warden. Then it was church twice a Sunday for me, with Sunday School and, later, Bible Class in the afternoons. This was a bit much, and eventually I dug my little toes in firmly, especially as I dimly realised that religion could never penetrate deeply into an Edwards. My mother was the only one in the household in whom a simple radiant faith burned steadily. She attended evensong only – she had to stay at home during matins to cook that Sunday dinner without which religion could not be sustained in my father and aunt.

Going to church, like the service itself, was a ritual. The importance given to Sunday clothes has implanted in me a lifelong distaste of formality in dress – I have never owned a topper, a bowler, morning clothes or an umbrella, and it must be all of forty years since I last got into a dinner jacket. Moreover, for the past quarter of a century I have emancipated myself from studs, cufflinks and detachable collars. The only exception was the occasion in 1961 when I had the privilege of taking Queen Elizabeth, the Queen Mother, around an exhibition. When I appeared in my war-paint, smelling faintly of mothballs, the Clerk of the Council exclaimed, "Good heavens, laddie, I didn't recognise you; you look respectable for once!" But on that memorable occasion I was acutely reminded of earlier days – of chafing Eton collars, tight shoes, pinching garters and those stiff cuffs, like fetters.

Armed with prayer books and collection money we set out in our sombre finery, down the street for one hundred and fifty yards, then up the causeway and into the churchyard – Father, Mother, Aunt Fanny, myself, my sister and, later, my cousin, now my brother-in-law. Fortunately, Dad liked being early for everything – and I take after him in this. We could sit in our pew half way up the nave and immediately behind the Vicar's Warden's pew (to which my Father eventually succeeded) and watch most of the congregation arrive. One could tell more about people when they pass through the south doorway than at any other time: one could sort out the elegant from the awkward, the arrogant from the humble, the hierarchy from the lowerarchy. This was important in an age when class mattered and the social range was not all that extensive. There was a brief exception when Lord Cardigan, the heir of the then Marquis of Aylesbury, came to live for a time at Cadbury House. He and his wife and his young family with their nanny would be ceremoniously ushered to the front pew immediately under the pulpit. I remember being shocked when his eldest boy, about my own age, marched to the pew with his topper still firmly on his head. He was just a little boy who had forgotten, but I thought him snooty. He certainly isn't – a year or so back I read an article about him (now the present marquis) which revealed him as a thoroughly nice chap, just like his father, who would occasionally come diffidently to our side door at night to buy some eggs for his bacon the next morning. This happened when they had run out – the aristocracy, even then in the golden evening of their glory, had their little local difficulties.

We were Low Church. When dear old Vicar Peart first arrived he bowed deeply towards the altar and we thought the Scarlet Woman was with us. Most of us walked straight to our pews without a glance eastwards. Some people nodded a sort of peck towards the altar; this was bad enough, but the very few who made a full genuflection were regarded by us with distaste and derision.

Matins was not too bad. I enjoyed the Te Deum, though, having mistaken a comma for a full stop, I was sorry for those perpetually weeping Cherubim and Seraphin, just as in the hymn I was sorry for the distant green hill which didn't have a city wall when all other hills had one. The Benedicite was funny: I thought of all those whales praising the Lord, and this business of 'magnifying' had a slightly different connotation for me. But when ante-communion replaced matins I became restless: there was too much going on inaudibly at the east end; indeed, it must have been hard work for any parson to be audible down the chancel, through the vault of the crossing and down the nave. The Litany was hell: perpetual kneeling, so that the pattern of the hassock became imprinted on my bare knees; a perpetual high-pitched gabble. That was the worst of being Low Church; nowadays I rarely miss hearing Tallis's Five Part on the radio – good old B.B.C.! Besides, nobody ever drew my attention to the superb words of the Litany; Shakespeare couldn't have done better. Incidentally, nobody ever explained simply that the Athanasian Creed was a careful, patient, early exercise in definition, casting a shaft of light on early and medieval ways of thinking. It should be used more often – it is much better than some of these interminable damned silly psalms about Og the King of Basan and dashing children against stones.

Evensong was much more cosy, especially if the psalms were not too long and we had any of my favourite hymns. Evensong at Easter, Whitsun and Harvest Festival was a treat, with its processional and recessional hymns. Instead of sidling in silently from the vestry in the south transept, the choir would move singing, through the open west door, right up the nave, and, eventually, back again: first the boys, then the men, with Uncle Jack Crease's tenor sounding like a golden trumpet, then the curate (when we had one) and finally the vicar with his hood (true Low Church, that!) – scarlet and black for Oxonian Vicar Wright, bunny rabbit for Dunelm Vicar Peart and resplendent D.C.L. trimmings for Vicar Dr. Browne, though I didn't know these important academic details at the time.

The sermon, though, was a bind; long by modern, though not by 17th century standards, far too long for any small boy. But though inattentive I was not idle – I came to know that remarkable agglomeration, the Book of Common Prayer. From the tables of Kindred and Affinity I learned precisely the women I couldn't marry; I juggled with the marvellous tables in the front and worked out when Easter would fall in 2000 A.D.; I knew how a bishop should be consecrated; I revelled in the commination service, that stark cursing match. My father, too, had reservations about sermons. Towards the end of my regular churchgoing days, when he was churchwarden, he always insisted on the south door remaining open on fine summer evenings. It was not until after his death that I learned the reason from George Hillman, a Congresbury man, who was about halfway in age between my father and myself and a friend of us both. It was an insurance against Vicar Peart riding his hobbyhorse, Socrates, throughout a sermon – Dad couldn't stand Socrates! At that time, evensong at Congresbury was an hour later than ours; Congresbury church lay a mile due south of ours; it had the finest peal of bells I have ever heard, and Dad could listen happily to them and ignore Socrates.

There is precious little about Chapel in this chapter. We were not ecumenical in those days; indeed, I have never been inside the Claverham or Horsecastle chapels and only once in the one in the High Street. But I had a good basinful of nonconformity when I stayed with Aunt Clara and Uncle Tom in Bath (see Chapter 14). However, at an early age I learned the rudiments of toleration. When I was about seven I went around shouting

> "Chapel bugs never agree,
> Hit their heads against a tree".

My mother admonished me, simply but firmly – "You shouldn't say things like that. Not everybody has had your advantage of a proper, Christian, Church of England upbringing. There are a lot of good people who go to chapel – quite a lot of good people. Take your Uncle Tom Coombe: where would you find a more honest, upright, Godfearing Christian man? – and he's a methodist, poor fellow".

When and why did the crunch come? – I am not sure. It has been said wisely that there is no such person as an agnostic – at the moment of truth one believes or one doesn't. I can recall occasions in childhood when I jibbed: when I first heard members of the Mothers' Union airing their venemous views on divorce; when my nonconformist kinsfolk were denouncing strong drink, forgetting about Cana in Galilee; when I stubbornly refused to be confirmed. It is easy to recall the *facts* of one's childhood, but difficult to remember exactly how one *thought* or *felt* at the time; the danger lies in antedating one's beliefs and disbeliefs. Perhaps I didn't feel, as I do now, that religion is a form of self-deception and an ever present barrier to truth. Perhaps my little childhood rebellions were nothing compared with the rage I felt, thirty-odd years ago, when that beastly archbishop kicked the Duke of Windsor when he was down and out – a nice spot of Christian charity, that was! I dislike the predestinates, the Calvins and Knoxes of this world; but perhaps there *is* no free will – perhaps belief or otherwise depends on the chemistry of one's make-up and is beyond our control. Indeed, I suspect that Englishmen as a whole (and certainly the Edwards tribe in particular) are not religious by nature, though not necessarily anti-religious; and once sanctions are eased and the priests are not on top, they slide into disbelief or, rather, into nothing in particular. Of course, there are plenty of exceptions among churchgoers and even among those who are not; and of course there is no substitute for religion, Christian or otherwise; humanism isn't, nor, I imagine, freemasonry and its various poor relations. I suppose cricket and communism come nearest. Those who are without the 'consolation' of religion are well aware of the fact.

At a lower level, I am grateful for an Anglican upbringing. In a boyhood spent in a village community, I was acutely aware of the gradations and importance of 'class'. Even today, I do not give much for this 'classless society' stuff, though I would like society to be organised not as a meritocracy in the socialist sense but on that old-fashioned conception of 'character'; the clever and successful people are not always the wisest. Perhaps the strongest old-fashioned prejudice which has survived from boyhood is the conviction that one can instantly tell an Anglican from most of the rest. The exceptions among the others are the Romans (after all, they were junior rivals in this land until the take-over deal in the 7th century) and the Friends, that band of renunciates and visionaries, who never in their three centuries of history could be termed a 'sect'. Otherwise, it is as easy as snap; and those who swap over either way cannot paint out their original spots.

But this is not relevant to the big question. Did I believe then as I suspect now that we are no more than transient dewdrops on the field of eternity? I cannot remember with any certainty. Anyhow, the main question may not be a teleological one – not, whither? It may well be – why did we come to exist? Why, oh why?

Chapter Eight

SWEET AUBURN TO ME

It is doubtful if even the most ardent local patriot could look on Yatton as the 'loveliest village of the plain'. For a matter of that, the loveliest villages are rarely found on plains: they are tucked into folds of the Cotswolds or rest within a rich golden-brown stone's throw of Ham Hill, or lie scattered over the rolling countryside of West Herefordshire and on either side of the Essex – Suffolk border. But even an exile far away can regard Yatton with fierce pride and a deep, burning affection.

The parish of Yatton is large, even though the civil and ecclesiastical parish of Cleeve was carved out of it in the 19th century. I am now far away from detailed Somerset reference books, but the one inch O.S. map, spread in front of me, shows that the parish is four and a half miles from the Brockley border in the E.N.E. to the Yeo River boundary in the W.S.W., and three miles from north to south. The main village street (with only a few offshoots in my boyhood) ran, and still runs, north-westwards right across the middle of the parish, and a good mile of this was built up well before my time. From the south end of the street, the hamlet of Claverham began, a winding road, a mile and a quarter long, but only built up solidly in isolated stretches. As its name indicates, the village was the 'gate town' at the northern fag-end of high land, guarding the way to Bristol north-eastwards and the Wrington Vale to the south-east. Cadbury Camp, at the extreme southern fringe of the parish, is two hundred and fifty feet high; the top of the village street is just above the fifty-foot contour; the bulk of the parish is marshland meadow, less than twenty feet above sea-level.

In my boyhood, the village was no beauty; it is less so nowadays, and has recently been called 'the largest village in Somerset', a very dubious compliment. The church is superb, magnificent (see Chapter 7); Rectory Farm, the old prebendal house, is a proud and dignified structure of *c*.1460; otherwise, there are only three or four buildings of any great architectural merit or interest. But I thought the village street was wonderful. I liked the way it sloped steadily downhill from The Score, where the road was cut through solid rock, to the railway station at its other end. I liked the long, straight stretches alternating with curves; I even liked the mud-coloured roughcast on many of the houses, necessary (though I didn't know it then) because most carboniferous limestone is porous and decidedly not first-class building stone. Above all, I liked its cleanliness, and when, at the age of about twelve, I found that Collinson, the Somerset historian, had thought

Proclamation of George V, 1910

so, too, a hundred years earlier, I was as proud as Lucifer.

But far more fascinating were the inhabitants and what they did. One of my early memories was the accession, proclamation and coronation of George V. The new king was proclaimed on the village green. Two postcards, now in front of me, depict the scene. In one of them, most heads are bowed. Obviously this was the point where we heard that it had pleased Almighty God to call his servant, Edward, from the world he had enjoyed so much – no more would that portly figure chase high-born ladies around the laurel bushes of Easton Lodge. In the other, heads were raised and all were listening intently; this was *the* moment – in a few seconds 'God Save the King' would ring out. A magnifying glass brings back memories. Old Mrs. Price is leaning on the gate of her 15th century home, Rectory Farm, the former Prebendal House; she still had several years to run. Ex-Colour-Sergeant Baber stands in front of his Church Lads' Brigade with their funny hats. Sidney Hill, J.P., is on the platform, looking even more self-important than he really was. The handsome face of the Vicar, Prebendary Roger Hayes Robinson, seems sad and pensive. My mother's young half-sister, Winnie, is there, with her 'Young Man', Gilbert Court; so, too, are Farmer William Burdge, Sam Sedgebeer, the railway man, and George Needham, the silver-haired builder and undertaker. Lots of little boys, one obviously a Stockham, but no sight of the little boy of five. He was there, though, hidden somewhere behind those long skirts and those wide hats like inverted washing-up bowls. Anyhow, a little later, I secured some mementos of the Coronation, or, rather, Aunt Fanny got them for me. I hadn't begun to go to Sunday school, but she marched into the church Sunday school and came out with a Coronation mug. Then she hustled me into the British Sunday school (that was Daniel in the Lions' Den, or *Athanasius contra mundum*) and wrested a Coronation medal from the dissenters.

Mixed up with the Coronation was my first political memory and act. At that time the village was deeply interested in national politics. My high Tory parents and aunt read and discussed all those columns of small print in the newspapers, particularly the vital debates in the Lords. I didn't know what it was all about, except that Lloyd George was a dirty word in our household, and there was sadness that Mr. Asquith, a proper gentleman in spite of his mistaken views, should threaten the House of Lords. But I did my part: at an election meeting on the village green, I threw a stone at the motor car of Joey King, the liberal candidate – there were young protesters sixty years ago!

Local elections did not come my way until the end of the period which this autobiography is supposed to cover. Previously, the parish council had usually been re-elected by show of hands at the parish meeting. But about 1919, when some new faces ventured to stand, Amy Avery, formidable Headmistress of Larchmount Hall School, created a sensation by jumping up at the meeting and declaring, 'I demand a poll'. In the weeks which followed, the candidates didn't quite know what to do. The parish clerk was kept busy; precedents were looked up; some candidates thought that canvassing was *infra dig*, and all those who were 'church' felt confident. The result was shattering. George Warburton, a quiet methodist and a genial, mild man, topped the poll. He was liked – and had no enemies; moreover, he was best placed for gentle canvassing he was the village postman! My father was well up: he had a handful of bitter enemies, but most people liked him. Some of the old hands were thrown out with a bump, and

Taffy Jenkins, the Welsh railwayman and erroneously held to be Bolshie, was elected. Then they all, the twelve victors and the seven or so defeated, made speeches from the raised front playground of the National School, much to the entertainment of the dense crowd – fully fifty! – in the street below. It was a riot. Even at that tender age I could recognise bad speeches – the poor dears, of course, had no practice or experience. One candidate was so inaudible that another candidate didn't realise he was speaking and embarked on his *apologia*. The only good speech came from Cuthbert Barnard one of the defeated, who had recently retired from his share of ruling India under the Queen-Empress and her successors.

Well before the First War, the fine, solid Church Hall was built, a tremendous corporate effort – even some of the chapel people helped. There were splendid fêtes in the Vicarage gardens with their giant ilexes and two large ponds – lakes, to my childhood eyes. Darcy Tripp raised quite a sum with his postcards, bearing a large circle, criss-crossed with thick and thin pencil lines and looking rather like a sieve designed by a lunatic; but when you held the card almost horizontally to your eyes and looked at it north-south, it read 'IN AID OF THE'. Then you turned it round, looked east-west, and the message was completed – 'NEW CHURCH HALL'. This everybody agreed, was 'real clever' of Darcy. Then somebody had the bright idea of having a printed book of quotations. You paid so much to have your little piece, original or otherwise, put in the book under the date of your birthday, with your name and address added. Then everybody bought the book to see what everybody else had inserted. A wonderful gossiping point, and money raised at both ends. Many of the inserts were hackneyed, biblical or sententious. Best of all, I liked 'Young Ben Crossman's. 'Young' Ben was a cheerful, extrovert farmer and a busy, bustling, match winning inside left. Alas, he has gone. Some years ago, I said, 'How's Young Ben Crossman getting on – still as vigorous as ever?" My nephew looked puzzled; then Alan said, 'Oh, you mean *Old* Ben; the poor old chap is crippled up with rheumatism'. I was sad: to me Ben Crossman meant the wonderful needle match on that crisp Boxing Day morning of 1919. Our opponents were Blackford, one of our only two near rivals in the Cheddar Valley League. It was a thrilling, end-to-end game, and we won, 4 – 2; but the decisive goal came from Ben's header, and it made the netting shudder. That Church Hall book is still somewhere in the depths of my boxroom, but I don't need to dig it out: Ben's doggerel, with its Somerset 'grammar' is firmly in my mind –

> 'On Claverham Rock, we did embrace,
> And then we stood, both face to face;
> The moon was up, the wind was high –
> I looked at she, and she at I'.

Football, yes! In the years just before and after the First War, our Lilywhites dominated the Cheddar Valley League. Only Blagdon and Blackford were anywhere in the same category, although, when it came to the knock-out Cup, the next village, Congresbury, often had the edge. All the Lilywhites were my heroes, and Jock Hilling, the goalie, was supreme; in my mind, he was bracketed with Sam Hardy of Aston Villa. They are nearly all gone. When I last enquired, Albert

Iles was alive. He was feared and closely-marked by our rivals; not always closely enough – he was the most elusive of centre-forwards. Several years ago, I was walking down the High Street and spotted Walter Smith on his bike – Walter, village blacksmith and staunch full-back. We chatted as if that thirty years since we last met was only yesterday. Then I said, "Play much football, nowadays, Walt?" The septuagenarian laughed; then he was silent, and his eyes gazed into infinity – he was back in the old days, fighting the old battles. Alas, he, too, has gone.

My cricketing days belong to the period following the time-span of this book. I was nine when cricketing packed up in 1914 for the Duration, as it was called. In the middle of the war, a cricketing devotee, too old for fighting, gave a talk on the rudimenta of the game to those of us who were members of Miss Coates's Boys Club, and I was horrified to discover that the game was played with a hard leather ball. They were all amused when I cried out, "But doesn't it *hurt*?" This was odd, because, when the time came, I proved to have sticky fingers. No good for a skier in the deep, but put me in close and I was like a chameleon catching flies. However, my initiation to this curious religion began just before 1919, the terminal date for this autobiography. You can't expect a mere trifle, like a world war, to stop disciples following their god; the old ones and the very young ones revived the Claverham Cricket Club, so that it should be a going concern when the warriors came home. 'Uncle' Jack Crease, a stalwart cricketer in the 1890s and the Edwardian era, led the revival. He was my favourite 'titular' uncle; he could talk cricket, a rare art, since most people who try to talk cricket end up by being insufferable bores. I learned about the traditions of Somerset and the local club, of Sammy Woods and Paliaret brothers; of W.G. coming down to the village and securing good batting practice in the nets by putting florins in the stumps instead of bails; of the legendary Tankerville Chamberlain, who sponsored representative matches in the village, ordered hindquarters of beef and whole lambs from the butcher; kept the baker baking overtime, ordered barrels of beer from the publicans, and then held open house throughout his cricket festival. Uncle Jack caused me to regard Albert Clapp with new respect. Albert was a harmless old boy, who pottered about the village, doing nothing much in particular, but Uncle Jack told me Albert had been a Somerset pro, and would have rivalled Len Braund if he hadn't been too prone to train on beer.

And what Uncle Jack didn't tell me, his son, 'Young' Jack, did. He was the leading batsman of the revived club, at first the only one who wasn't old or a mere boy. He had been badly wounded in 1917 and invalided out of the army, but by 1918 he was just fit enough to take up the game he had last played as a public schoolboy in 1914. He is about eight years my senior, but I still think of him as 'Young' Jack, I suppose because his father is still so deeply engraved in my memory and affection. Appropriate, too – 'Young' Jack is far and away the most youthful-looking septuagenarian I've ever seen.

For the first few years, the revived club played on an indifferent field before returning about 1920 to their original ground and rising to their former eminence under the captaincy of R. L. Gosling. In 1919 I was no more than a spectator, but one day, when they were short-handed, I was conscripted and became a dogsbody at point until a fullblooded slash came hurtling towards me. "Shape to it, boy", they shouted; but I stood still until the last second, just held my left hand out, and the ball stuck. They couldn't get over this – "Thought you were asleep, boy"; but they began to take some notice of me from that moment.

The most important village event was the annual Flower Show and Fête held in the two fields at The Score, rented by my father. As the tenant's son, I was the only non-participant who had a free pass, and I used to stroll around with a proprietorial air. It was probably very little different from thousands of others up and down the country, but to me it was special, held in *our* fields. One field contained the lesser tents, the side shows and the huge, main tent with the exhibits, plus that mingled smell of trampled grass and greengrocer's shop. The other field was used for afternoon sports and displays. But I cannot say that it left more than two or three deep impressions. Perhaps the one which remains most clearly is not of the show itself, but the prelude – the incalculable amount of work which went into its making, the consultations among friendly rivals, the mean-spirited nastiness and jealousy among the few, causing some anxious competitors to stay up all night just before the show to guard their precious specimens from theft or mutilation. Is there similar intensity and solidarity in horticultural shows nowadays? Are there still specialists – the runner bean bloke, for example, who digs his trenches halfway to New Zealand, rams old socks and pieces of flannel in the bottom, fills up steadily with nauseous animal blood and vegetable decay, and then, in due season, lovingly slips his beans into lampglasses to ensure straightness and length? I hope so, but perhaps there are no lampglasses nowadays. And as for onions, well, growing them for show is an applied art of great delicacy and skill.

Perhaps the most lively juvenile organisation in the village was the Scout troop. I don't share the modern view that Scouts are knobbly-kneed Peter Pans and I rather regret the modernisation of the uniform devised by Baden-Powell; but, then, I regret the death of Imperialism, the rise of the Common Man, the lowering of academic standards and a large number of other manifestations of decline in the West. I enjoyed my two years as a Scout; I was proud of my Tenderfoot badge and looked forward to imminent rise to Second Class and ultimate ascent to First Class – why, although a mere tenderfoot, I had knocked back the requirements for the Naturalist badge and was seeking new worlds to conquer. What a pity the new Scoutmaster had no understanding of little West Country rustics; he killed it all stone dead in a few months. I have never cared much for discipline, apart from self-discipline and the discipline which used to be associated with academic study, but I reckon that the Scout Movement offered the best kind of imposed discipline – it offered young boys all that was good in the way of ordered life; it gave scope for ritual and dressing-up and opportunity for learning useful skills. Moreover it was free from some of the crass stupidities of militarism. Anyhow, I've kept my tenderfoot badge!

Recollection is a disorderly exercise. The past comes back readily enough, but not as pieces of a jig-saw puzzle which can be put together again; more like a flutter of falling petals – and you can't put 'em back on the rose. Not that village life ever was like a rose. A rose is a unity; the village of Yatton in my boyhood was a collection of nearly two thousand individual souls, all endowed with free-will – at least, one hopes so, for if that is not true, then there is no hope. As a small boy, I knew only a fraction of what was going on in the minds and lives of the two thousand, and only a fraction of that fraction has survived. But if I had known and retained all that there was to know, it would be impossible to create a unity out of that knowledge. Life is one thing, and art is quite another. All one can do is to recall something which concerned everybody and gave some semblance of unity. Church? – no! There were the dissenters, the few Roman Catholics and those who had no religion. Farming? – no! A small, isolated village, with its agricultural workers and its specialist tradesmen, could be regarded as something of a unity. But we had the railway, Wake and Dean's furniture factory, Court de Wyke Tannery, the commuters to Bristol and Weston-Super-Mare, and their opposites, the retired townsfolk seeking a rural old age.

Perhaps the weather was a great unifying force. It mattered to the whole village, not merely to those engaged in farming. It mattered to me, a small village boy. It matters to me now in my trade as a tenth-rate local historian – soil and meteorology are behind geography, and geography is behind history, and three cheers for Professor Hoskins! How wise of the B.B.C. to turn the met boys and the met girl on to the great British public. I love their voices, most of them regional and unspoilt, even though one chap puts it on a bit and sounds like George Brown. That attractive Welsh voice; the Australian voice, regarded with nation-wide affection and now, alas gone back home, and that voice which sounds a little like mine, but perhaps a trifle to the north – is it Somerset-Gloucestershire borders or Forest of Dean? Others share my joy: just before Rosea went back to Australia, I overheard a comment which warmed my heart – "Going to be fine today, Jim, Rosie said so."

Long ago, Dad was my Rosea, though not as good-looking. He just smelt the air and sniffed. The morning sun would shine from a cloudless sky, but he would say, "Take your mac; you'll need it before the day is out". Morning rain would cause despondency – I had looked forward to a day among the butterflies – but he would say, "It will clear up in an hour or so". He was always right. Seasoned rustics who knew all about swallows, smoke and the way cattle face, would seek and respect his judgment. Perhaps it was akin to his prowess as a dowser. Gloomy organisers on the eve of the village Fête, would look at the heavy clouds and say, "Bad for the feet," Dad would sniff and say, "Don't worry, it will be all right by the morning".

There seemed to be more extremes of weather when I was young. Torrential winter rains would flood the marshlands. Once, there was a sudden change; the flood waters froze, and the price of skates rose. The experts could skate in a straight line to Nailsea, turn and come back, a matter of eight miles. To my sorrow, I was considered to be too young to be allowed on the ice, but most people had a marvellous time, except nice, portly, deaf Mr. Tutt, the grocer – he went through! He was in no danger, but he took quite a deal of retrieving.

Exact dates are not clear in my mind. There was the snowy winter, when drifting completely covered the large, sitting room window, and early lambs, rescued from field drifts, were restored by my mother in front of the kitchen fire. This started her off: she rivetted me with her story of the great blizzard of her girlhood when they searched for sheep deep in drifts and were guided by faint yellow discoloration caused by sheep breath rising slowly through fifteen feet of snow. Then she got on to stories, told by her grandfather, of snowy winters long before Victoria became queen.

There was that wet summer during the First War, when 'Uncle' John Burdge didn't get his hay harvest in until mid-October – not very good hay! There was the glorious summer a few years earlier when the long, fine spell was broken by a couple of conveniently-spaced, adequately heavy showers which prolonged and bountified the strawberry harvest, Royal Sovereigns for weeks on end, the most appropriately named of all strawberries. They are difficult to obtain nowadays. All sorts of excuses are made: they are not good croppers for this age of profitability; they are difficult to raise, like young turkeys. Bah! – mankind doesn't know what is good for it. A pre-First-War breakfast out-of-doors in the cool brightness of 7 a.m. Dispense with eggs and bacon for once; instead, a huge dish of Royal Sovereigns in the middle of the table; ladle a young mountain of caster sugar on your own plate; thin bread-and-butter in the left hand; a strawberry held by its stem in the right hand; bite the tip off and then rub the strawberry round and round in the caster sugar. Keep on keeping on, and watch the caster sugar acquire its carmine tinge, like blood on the snowy field of Borodino.

No, the weather really mattered in our village. A few years ago, I heard a New-Statesman-type sophisticate denouncing country bumpkins – "Their only conversation is the weather". Poor chap; he didn't realise that the weather is the great unifying bond. Wouldn't those old dears, dead these fifty years and more, have loved to switch on at 6.55 a.m. and pass on the good news – "Going to be fine today, Jim – Rosie said so".

Chapter Nine

EARLY SCHOOLS

That early illness seems to haunt this book. Not that I remember much about it, apart from feeling rather dim and miserable. but it seemed to have turned a bright little chap of four into a dull and backward boy of seven. I've been a late developer ever since: fancy not writing a first (unpublished) novel until one's sixty-fourth year – sensible people get that folly over in their university days.

Anyhow, no school until about three weeks after my sixth birthday. My parents began by taking me to Larchmount Hall, run by the indomitable Miss Amy Avery, and proud of its reputation throughout the West of England. But I cried my eyes out and didn't last more than half a day. Then they sent me to Yatton High School, next door but one to Larchmount Hall. It was owned and dominated by old Miss Crease, though run by Miss Holbrook and Miss Taylor. I wore a broad-brimmed straw hat, with a band of black-and-white stripes and Y.H.S. woven on it, and continued to be moderately miserable. The trouble was that I was lost, just as lost as the succession of Mam'selles, varied by one Fraulein, who tried to teach me French before I was aware of the rudiments of English. I didn't understand what was going on, and generally nobody troubled to explain. Take music, for example – I had always assumed I was tone deaf, though a few years ago my colleague, Eric Stapleton, the Essex County Music Adviser, assured me that I'm not, but there is a blockage somewhere – I can never be certain of keeping to the right key, and I'm quite incapable of translating tonic-solfa or those damned pothooks on lines into the correct sounds. This is a matter for mirth nowadays, but think of the terror it induced in a seven-year-old. There was a nauseating little thing called the Japanese Fan Dance. Three of us had to sing it and make silly motions with our fans. The old girl at the piano (I forget her name) would play, but my voice couldn't hit the notes. I used to be kept in for after-school bouts at this song, but in the end she gave up and said I was the naughtiest and stupidest boy she had ever known. Not *just* – I was a very unnaughty boy, and even in those days of retarded progress I knew I wasn't stupid.

There was another source of terror. The main schoolroom was also used as a Sunday School by the United Methodist Chapel next door. The Chapel is a mid-to-late Victorian affair, but the schoolroom is much older – I haven't been inside it for many years, but, looking back, I'm certain it must be late Georgian. anyhow, it had a gallery, a dusty, rarely used gallery, and this was the place of banishment for naughty boys. I dreaded the possibility of being sent to it, even though Jim Lewis didn't seem to mind frequent spells there; when Miss Holbrook wasn't looking, he would lean over the top and make faces at the rest of us down below.

Yatton High School came to an end when I was eight. 'Madame' Langdon, who had succeeded old Miss Crease, decided to leave the village. The boarders all wept as they said goodbye to us little day boys, and I was sent to the British School, one of the village's two elementary schools.

Presumably, it still had some connection with the British and Foreign School Society, but it had an even older Quaker origin in the early 18th century. Its correct title was Yatton Undenominational School, and its managers headed by Farmer William Burdge, were leading village nonconformists. Old William Burdge, side-boarded, grave in face, kindly in manner, was a pillar of rectitude. He always looked so neat and clean; his black suit was speckless, his linen was snowy white. He was a widower, with an enormous family, then ranging from the under forties to the late fifties; all of them, except Richard, lived to a good age. I always liked Old William's visits to the school. They gave me a sense of assurance – my family were on friendly terms with most of the Burdges, and vaguely connected with them by marriage. Besides, John, the best of the lot, was my titular uncle. They all had 'character', that priceless virtue – outmoded today – which is difficult to define and easy to recognise. Tom Burdge, for instance, was solid and dependable; he had a dry wit, and a curious action as a slow bowler. He was the slowest driver of a car I have ever seen, and was always getting into minor accidents. We used to tell him that if he drove faster he would pass the scene of an accident before he had one.

Miss Brentnall was 'Governess'; she was rather like a stern but kindly turkey cock. Maud Radbourne taught the juniors; Mrs. Davies ruled over the infants' room. Of course, Maud was officially 'Miss Radbourne' to me, but I always thought of her as 'Maud', as she was a local girl and lived with her widowed mother near my home. Mrs Davies was a cheerful Welsh widow with two children, Percy and Beatrice. Beatie was my senior by one day; we shared a twin desk, and I thought she was wonderful. Recently, with my thoughts far away, as usual, I popped into the village post office. Normally, post office ladies tend to be a little frosty; so I was startled by a friendly, cheerful voice, still with a trace of that Welsh lilt. It was Beatie, as vivacious as ever – Albert Pearce was a lucky man when he married her well over forty years ago.

I was still dim at eight, but I began to learn, and even won a prize for general progress and had my clay model of Julius Caesar's head put in the glass case, known as The Museum. Not the rapid progress I was to make under the Gaffer (see Chapter 10), but enough for me to be aware of it. I cannot remember much about the actual teaching, but I do recall my first interest in history. Maud Radbourne used to read us a chapter from 'the book', say, the Battle of Hastings and all that led up to it. Then she would pass the book around the class so that we could see the pictures; then she would question us. I suppose educationalists would call this pretty primitive teaching, but quite honestly, as a retired County History Adviser, I don't see much wrong with it, and probably Socrates would have approved. It gave me the romance of it all – the wall of shields, with the Dragon of Wessex and the Fighting Man waving above them; that arrow in the eye; the last desperate struggle before the survivors broke and fled into the dusk. At least, I was given a catholic selection of stories and could follow some of them up in Herbert Strang's books, which were used as 'readers'; enough for any small boy. Old hat? – Well, I wonder! Recently, one of my colleagues questioned a group of juniors visiting Ingatestone Hall; their knowledge of history stories was confined to Dick Whittington and Lenin!

My scattered memories are few: fear of His Majesty's inspectors; girls with nits in their heads; Ida Short going berserk whenever there was a thunderstorm; my protracted conflict with Reggie Wilmot. Why we fought, I cannot remember, but it went on savagely day after day. Then I got the upper hand; then his big brother thrashed me; then my cousin thrashed him. Then it stopped, probably because there wasn't anyone around big enough to thrash my cousin.

The building was interesting, not intended for the school, which had moved there just before I came to it. It was built in the mid-Victorian age by the Society of Friends, then far more numerous in the area. There were only two classrooms, but they were large, tall, light and airy. The Quakers, those quiet, peaceful visionaries, retained a long, narrow side room, and occasionally they met there during school hours. I could see them going in and out, but I never heard them. Pity there aren't more of them around nowadays; the world could do with a few quiet people. They had a graveyard there, beside the playground. It was small, carefully tended and only once used during my time there for the burial of Old Peckitt's wife; and they lined the hole with trails of ivy leaves. I liked that graveyard; it didn't seem to invoke any fear. Maybe I liked it because those inscriptions on the plain stones were too short for maudlin sentiments – certainly too short for lies!

Chapter Ten

THE GAFFER

Long ago, in the mid-winter of 1927-28 – I cannot recall the day or month – I phoned from Bristol to my mother at home. Before I could give her my message, she said, "I have some sad news for you: poor Mr. Mansey has died very suddenly." I knew then that I had lost my best friend. I know now that he had a deeper influence on me than any other man, except possibly George Hare Leonard.

Hugh Mansey was short and podgy, with streaks of heavily pomaded hair eked out across his bald head. He had prominent cod's eyes, an amorphous pink nose with distended pores, yellow fangs, a straggly drooping moustache and an oddly-deformed index finger; and I loved him more than any other man except my Uncle Ted. He was the first of the three outstanding schoolmasters I have known over the years. He hadn't the intellect of that mathematician and visionary, Charles Wilfred Tregenza, or that Wellington-like sense and sensibility of Philip Whitting, but, like those two, he could teach superbly; and short of possessing the genius of a Shakespeare or a Newton that is the greatest gift any man can have.

Unlike every potential field marshal, he did not keep his baton in his knapsack; he taught with it. It was a piece of wood about eighteen inches long, originally oblong in section but with two edges planed off to a semi circle and the other two still very much there. It was his ever present pointer and cane. If a culprit's offence was merely technical he got the rounded side across his outstretched hand; the really naughty boys got one of the sharp edges. His use of this handy little weapon would horrify modern educationalists, the poor silly clots. He caned boys fairly frequently (and girls only very occasionally) for being stupid and making mistakes in their work. The technique was always the same: he would sit down on the bench beside the victim, but facing towards him. Then the interrogation would begin: he would go right to the root of the error, explaining carefully by way of question and answer exactly where the boy had gone wrong and exactly what he should have done to avoid his folly. If the boy did not understand, he would go over it again using simpler terms. Only when perfect understanding was reached would the moment of reckoning come – you held out your hand, and down came that bit of wood with just enough force to sting, but no more.

For a serious offence the interrogation was longer and the caning more severe. Sometimes the culprit was made to write out his offence (not a bad training in narrative prose work) and this was then pasted into the log book. There was the affair of Sid Ford, who, poor lad, was drowned a few years later, bathing in Little River. Sid's examination lasted, on and off, from mid-morning to mid-afternoon, and though I kept my nose in my book and listened eagerly, I could not gather the exact offence. Years later my father and I were going through the logbook, and there was that scrap of pasted-in paper with the account in Sid's spidery hand. It began:

> BUGER
> I said this to Mrs. Walker over the
> playground wall . . . .

Another boy, I remember, kissed a girl and her father complained. This caused another long inquisition and a short, sharp caning. Memories like these show how far we have travelled educationally over the past fifty years – but in which direction? In my later schoolmastering days, in the 1940s, I realised that most forms of punishment were just plain daft and time-wasting, especially any variant of the so-called imposition. The only thing wrong with Mansey's methods was that long interrogation; indeed, the only effective punishment, to my mind, is to tell a boy to bend over promptly and apply a gym slipper to the seat of his intelligence.

But that little stick of Hugh Mansey's also epitomised the other side of that wonderful little man. It waggled all day long; it conducted the morning hymn; it pointed to the blackboard; it banged the blackboard; it came down with a wallop on the front row of desks; it pointed accusingly at a slightly inattentive boy in the back row; it went up and down the modulator; it beat time to a class recitation of 'Breathes there the man whose soul's so dead'; it waved joyously through a rendering of 'Tom Bowling', emphasising the aspirates; it unhooked diagrams from the walls; and then, exhausted, at 3.30 p.m., it went to sleep on Gaffer's desk next to the india rubber, the ruler and the red ink pen for the register.

Mansey ruled over an Anglican empire. The National School looked southwards across the small village green to the stately 15th century Prebendal House, now Rectory Farm, on the other side. The great church stood on the west side of the green. Mr. Harris's house and garden ran along the east side, or at least it was Mr. Harris's during my short time at the school; earlier it had been Mr. Pidgeon's, but, alas, he fell off his roof and died. It was an early National School, with the date, 1834, still clearly visible under its front gable. Those who cut the date had no idea of the wheat fields which would grow from that little £20,000 seed planted by Lord Grey's government. They didn't know about the tares, either – or, perhaps, one should say, the wild oats.

There were only three classrooms: the infants were in one, Standards I and II in another; the big room, divided by a partition, housed Standards III to VII. There was a small playground in the front, another at the back and a large one on the opposite side of the road. The one battered washbowl in the boy' cloakroom lacked its plug, and the privies stank vilely. But the classrooms were tall, well-warmed by Tortoise stoves and well-ventilated by tall, wide windows. Those outmoded windows should be commended to the glass-box, light-level experts in the Department of Education and Science and to all school architects; they let in adequate light, but they were set high enough in the wall to shelter youngsters from most of the direct heat of the summer sun. They were also good for concentration – they prevented the little blighters from looking out. Classrooms are surely meant for the job in hand; they are not intended to be gazebos.

The Gaffer's desk stood on a platform in front of one long wall of the big room, and near the partition. He could look straight down on Standard V, with the few members of VI and VII behind them. A yard or so to their right was Standard IV; at least, they were there when they were not doubled up with Standard III. Standard III lived beyond the partition to the Gaffer's right; they were Miss Brown's little pigeons. Sometimes there was a student teacher; but usually Mansey and Miss Brown coped with what was virtually half the school. Nobody, least of all the two teachers, ever thought there was anything unusual or understaffed about this. Teaching was then a full-time job; there were no 'free' periods; marking and preparation were done after school hours, and no teacher ever did his prep more thoroughly than Hugh Mansey. He knew that teaching was an infinite capacity for taking pains.

He showed that infinite capacity on the day of my arrival at the late age of eleven years and four months. He gave me a few sums to do and a writing test, and then went on with his teaching. When I had finished, he came over and sat down beside me. The sums were right and so was the content of the writing test. 'Yes', he said, 'but we expect something a bit better here. Look at this long division. What's the name for that bit, the answer? Yes, the quotient. Now, why not put these figures along the top, like this, and make 'em small. And look at that big, thick, round rolling writing all over the place. Think of the waste – and with those sprawling long division sums. This paper belongs to the Somerset County Council, and your father helps to pay for it – you'll have us all bankrupt.' I didn't quite know what bankrupt meant, but he was chuckling; so my errors could not have been too bad or caneworthy. Then he showed me how to do the standard Elementary School Hand of that period – 'Don't mind about lifting the pen; your job is to get the shapes right first; *then* you can keep the pen down all the time'. All this may seem trifling, but it was important to me; it was probably the first time I had been given a piece of positive, personal, constructive teaching. And I am grateful to him for teaching me that long-derided, angular Elementary Hand. Many men and women of sixty and seventy still write that way, and they are *legible;* but the point is that it is probably the best training from which a good, cursive individual hand can develop. Don't give me that stuff about italic writing. Italic is lovely as a formal hand, but no more. Years ago, I went to a Victoria and Albert exhibition of the great Edward Johnston's writing; everybody praised it, but I thought his cursive italic was pretentious and illegible. Italic is no go the Yogi man as a basis for ordinary writing; anyhow, it is a revival, and I dislike revivalism in all its forms – Strawberry Hall Gothic, Sankey and Moody, Oxford Movement, Tea Shoppe Tudor and Old Uncle Banker's Georgian and all.

From that day, Mansey took perpetual pride and delight in my progress. I didn't think I was ever Teacher's Pet; if I had been, the other boys would certainly have given me a rough handling. It was, I suppose, that I was the answer to a schoolmaster's prayer – a retarded boy who longed to listen and learn and goggled at the wonder of the vistas being unfolded for me. Looking back, I realise that he was the ideal teacher at the right moment. At the time, I quickly became aware of his humanity and humility, and thus, of his limitations. He was a leader, not a master, a beckoner, not a driver, wise but not omniscient. He never pretended: if he didn't know the answer he said so frankly; if he thought the missing bit of knowledge was important, he would say, "I think I have a book which will tell us the answer. I'll look it up; you ask me again tomorrow". I have even known him to pop out of school to his house next door and come back quickly with a book wide open and an ugly grin on his ugly face – "Come here, laddie, here it is, here it is". But he was not a bookish man; he was not at all academic, he was not intellectual; and I often wonder if his influence is responsible for my own aversion to men who cannot write a paragraph without recourse to footnotes, *op. cit, loc. cit, infra, ibid* and all the other trappings of pedantry. In fact, he was a trained, certificated teacher – and, in his day, they didn't push 'em past *that* hurdle regardless. Moreover, he had a certificate in drawing (would it be what I think was called the Art Teacher's Certificate?). Anyhow, not many village schoolmasters fifty-odd years ago had that combination of qualifications.

Fifty years ago, his teaching methods must have been pretty unusual. I am not certain about this and have never bothered to find out; all I can say is that I was the eager recipient of them. Probably he did not get them out of books; probably he did not know the terms 'correlation' and so forth given to them by educationalists; possibly he did not learn them at college. He was a natural: he taught about what he knew, what he believed in, above all, what he saw. He would do his homework when bits of detail were needed, but generally he taught off the cuff. It was visual teaching which flowed from his whole being; it was his way of expounding by words, pictures and deeds the unity of knowledge he found in nature around him.

Looking back across the years, it is difficult for me to find the starting point of his teaching. Some memories are as clear as a raindrop; some are so cloudy that it is hard to distinguish honestly between what he actually did and any ideas he may have sparked off in me. But it is probably true to say that his was *circular* teaching: the writing of English was not its starting point, but it is a convenient point at which to break into the circle. Every little essay was well prepared and expounded to the class, orally, in writing on the blackboard (with paragraph headings carefully underlined) and visually by clear and careful little blackboard sketches. Then we wrote the essays in our books and copied the sketches, but it wasn't a mere repetition exercise – we were encouraged to write down anything relevant which we knew and was not on the blackboard; and if we could produce any variant of his sketches, or, rarely, any quite original drawing, he would become excited – 'Stop, all of you. Look, this is good . . . . if you haven't gone too far, see if you can put in something like it'.

Most of these puny little essays sprang from Nature. We wrote on Clouds, and the clumsier boys and girls made blots trying to put heavy shading on sketches of a nimbus-covered sky. We wrote about Fungi, poisonous and edible, and I grew ultra-cautious when picking mushrooms in the early morning. We wrote about Migration of Birds and drew dotted lines on little sketch maps to show their routes; and he would call us slow-coaches if he saw a spring swallow back from Africa before we did. He would carefully dissect regurgitated owl pellets, show us the ingredients of a predator's dinner, draw them on the blackboard, and then set us to write it all down.

Many of the essays came from his love of gardening. He had decent sized plots at the front and back of the school house; but in that U-boat era of 1917-18 he took on a large allotment and yearly won second prize. Mr. Kench, the railway guard, always had first prize with his ultra-tidy, heavily-groomed plot. This worried me: a man who not only taught gardening in school, but also taught other teachers how to teach gardening was a superman and should rightly be first. Rather fearfully I raised this. Mansey was pleased with the implied flattery; he chuckled merrily and said, "Now, laddie, I always insist on you boys being *tidy* gardeners and I keep my own garden tidy, but an allotment is different. I like it to look decent, but this is a war effort. I *grow* potatoes there, I don't mollycoddle them and wipe the tears from their eyes. I'm quite content to be second to Mr. Kench". Then came that hideously ugly grin, followed by a big ho-ho-ho of a chuckle – "but I could beat him if I set my mind to it."

Gardening began in the classroom. We were taught the theory of it from asparagus to zinnias; our exercise books were full of little essays and sketches on double-digging, capillary attraction, rotation of crops, Bordeaux mixture and pruning. One afternoon a week Standards I and II swapped places with us and their room was turned into a woodwork shop. Bench-tops with vices were clamped to the tops of desks. Out of a cupboard came jack planes, smoothing planes, saws, chisels, try-squares, spokeshaves and the rest. We produced the drawings we had made of dibbles, seed potato carriers, and those fan-like contraptions placed at either end of a row of seedlings and then joined by strands of cotton; there were isometric drawings, plans, elevations, side views, details of joints, the lot. Then we made these bits and pieces of gardening aids, and they had to be well made otherwise that other little bit of wood with its two sharp edges would be used by the Gaffer.

The school gardens lay on the other side of the main playground, at a higher level and screened by a wall. This was an advantage: if we were fooling around we could usually spot the Gaffer approaching before he could see us. Once we were nearly caught out; we just managed to get back to our plots and grasp spade or fork before his head appeared coming up the steps – that is, all of us except Joe. He had to pop into the rhubarb forcing box and pull the lid down. Mansey made no comment on Joe's absence. He moved amiably around from plot to plot, encouraging, admonishing, discussing. Finally, after half an hour, he said, "Now, boys, I think we all ought to see how the rhubarb is getting on". We followed obediently, and the Gaffer lifted the lid. Up rose a cold, stiff, terrified Joe. Mansey tried to simulate wrath, but he couldn't. He laughed until he cried, and he went on laughing at intervals all the rest of the afternoon.

There were fourteen of us gardeners, a senior and a junior to each of the seven plots. To be promoted to the fourteen was the ambition of every boy in the school. As well as the seven gardens, there were the soft fruit plots – redcurrants, blackcurrants and gooseberries – a tool-shed and a well. Any boy caught climbing down into the half-empty well was promptly caned, and rightly so – Joe in the rhubarb box was a joke, but the Gaffer wasn't going to have any drowned boys on his register. On our own plots we grew one row of nearly every kind of vegetable, and grew them well; even our parents had to admit this. After all, if a plot of land is well-manured, dug and double dug, forked, raked to a silky tilth, carefully sown, hand-weeded, Dutch-hoed, watered and lovingly watched by two boys and an exacting master, it certainly ought to grow good stuff. The spoils were fairly divided – Mansey had one third, we shared the other two. All of us, in turn, pruned and tended the fruit bushes; the Gaffer would take all the gooseberries one year, the redcurrants the next year, and so on; we all shared the remainder. This was certainly fair, especially as I happened to know, through my father, that some of the 'extras' in the way of running costs came out of the Gaffer's own pocket; but I used to wonder how he, Mrs. Mansey, Harold, his son, and little Lilian his daughter, could knock back all that amount of produce, plus all he grew at the back of his house and on his allotment. Long afterwards I discovered that poor old widows, living on their own, could often reckon on a couple of juicy cos lettuces or a bunch of fresh carrots.

Sometimes things went wrong. One of us would say "Sir, blackfly, I think", or, "those plants don't seem to be doing well". He would come quickly, his face grave, and pull up three or four plants – "Ha tap-root". He would gather us around him and give a short lesson on the spot. Next day we would find the blackboard full of drawings. A succinct lecture followed, and then we took down everything in our exercise books. By 1919, I must have made a drawing of every possible garden bug as seen under a microscope; and Mansey didn't crib all of these from books – he had his own microscope.

The gardens came directly into the art lessons; we grew fine vegetables, but we also had to draw them. This was good education; you were proud of that bunch of four beetroots on your desk, and you felt bound to do them justice in watercolours. Justice meant being as life-like as possible – that superb teacher of drawing was a rigid representationalist. He taught us, or tried to teach us, every trick he knew – even today, I find myself holding out a pencil upright at arm's length to gauge the relative heights of tall objects. He would say, 'That box you've drawn, boy, is standing on a point. Did you ever see a box stand on a point? Make it sit down. Hold your pencil out dead level, both hands. Bring it to the nearest point of the box. Now, what angle does the left hand side make with your pencil? 25°? You've made it about 60° Now then, how often have I said that upright lines always appear upright except when you are looking up at the church tower over there." Then again, "Parallel lines never meet; but you go down to the station and look at the straight stretch of the line towards Puxton." The new vicar's wife fancied herself as an artist. She wasn't, though her daughter was an extremely sensitive and accomplished one. The old girl did a water-colour drawing of the church, and for years it hung in the vestry. Mansey regarded it with derision; it aroused that odd noise which is half way between a chuckle and a ho-ho-ho – a chortle, I suppose: "Laddie, I shouldn't be saying this to you, but look at it, look at it. She has no more idea of perspective than that surplice – she can't draw." She couldn't.

Art he loved, and next to art, nature. Those nature rambles were part of that circular, revolving way of teaching which emphasised the unity of knowledge, though I am pretty sure he did not think about it consciously in that way. With Lilian clinging to one arm and one of her girl friends on the other, he would gaily lead us off across the fields to Brockley Combe, a good cross-section of countryside, from marshy rhynes with cuckooflower on their rims to limestone crags with yew trees in their fissures. There was plenty for everybody, from fungi to fossils. I was never much good at bird recognition, though there were boys who were capable of holding their own with the Gaffer, and they did, to his great pleasure. It was when an unusual butterfly crossed our path that I became the proud expert.

Birds and butterflies – it was Mansey's lesson on butterflies and his own collection which really fired me. Throughout 1917, 1918 and 1919 I acquired the best schoolboy's collection in the village and even began to breed them, though my mother disapproved of caterpillars galloping around my bedroom, seeking a quiet corner in which to pupate. Now, in early old age, I am thinking about returning to butterflies – I shall breed them but not kill them. They made me realise a salient point in the Gaffer's character, one which contributed deeply to his pre-eminence as a teacher. This was his modesty, his repudiation of omniscience. If a boy could genuinely display superior knowledge and prove him wrong, he was utterly delighted – those boys, for instance, who could beat him at bird recognition. In his collection he had misnamed one of the butterflies. I spotted this, but it was a good week before I could steel myself to mention it. He listened carefully as I went over the differences, the little markings on the underwings, point by point. "You're right", he said, "You're absolutely right." But he didn't leave it at that; his error didn't worry him, but the fact that one of his boys had the knowledge to discover it had to be joyfully announced to the whole class.

The afternoon of Ascension Day, a half-holiday, was always a nature ramble time. But there was the morning treat too. As the school was C. of E. we all trooped over to a service in the church. Then everybody, from Standard IV upwards, symbolically ascended the church tower. This was a treat indeed: the whole world lay before us – the Mendips to the south, Cadbury Hill and Kingswood to the east, Clevedon and its hills to the north and, to the west, across the alluvial plain, the silver line of the Bristol Channel. Below lay the village, fully exposed, even down to Mrs. Viney's washing on the line. Then came the special joy; the older boys and girls went higher, up the ladder to the top of the pepperpot, the truncated spire. Here one could almost touch the surprisingly large gilded weathercock. Better still, we were literally one up – we could look down with disdain on the youngsters lining the quite roomy parapet of the tower.

Although his greatest personal skills lay in drawing and the crafts, the Gaffer was probably at his happiest when teaching geography. I don't think he had ever travelled much; how could a poor usher with a wife, two kids and a position to maintain be expected to travel on a pre-Burnham pittance! But he knew his world and travelled accurately all over it on the wings of his mind. He hadn't heard of Visual Aids, but he used them extensively over fifty years ago, and when he couldn't find a picture or lantern slide, there was always his active pencil or stick of chalk. He taught and transported us imaginatively; his magic carpet was woven with materials he had accumulated – cotton pods from Egypt, flax for Irish linen, jute from India, the fine fibres of a kashmir shawl. As always we drew like mad, and one boy even made a more-or-less working model of a shaduf on the Nile.

Out of school Mansey was a little aloof, though sociable enough when approached. I think he was conscious of his position: he didn't go into pubs, he didn't drink; I cannot remember if he smoked, but I think not; he wasn't a thruster or a joiner. He was very much a family man. His wife was quiet, sweet-natured and valetudinarian, though she lived to an advanced age. His daughter, Lilian, petite and fragile and adored by her father, survived him by only a year or so. His son, Harold, was cheerful and open-natured, but not clever. Indeed the only defect I ever found in Mansey was obvious enough – he was disappointed in Harold's lack of academic ability and was far, far too severe with him. He rarely entertained, but every year, the bigger boys looked forward to their invitation to Harold's birthday party. Here that well-known ho-ho-ho was given full play, though even on that day Harold rarely escaped a scolding.

However, like many quiet, unassuming men, the Gaffer led an active extra-mural life. In those days, the secretaryship of the Parochial Church Council virtually went with the headmastership of a village C. of E. School; and when there was a gap between curates, Mansey would fill in as Superintendent of the Sunday School, or take the evening services at the Claverham mission church. Every year, with the Head of Long Ashton village school, he ran a Saturday morning course in handicraft and gardening for village heads in the district. Every winter, helped by Harry Rattle, the water engineer, he ran a night school on Monday and Tuesday evenings.

As a schoolboy I was ineligible to join night school, but Mansey was not going to allow regulations to bar a little glutton for learning; he enrolled two of us boys as monitors. Every Monday and Tuesday, after school, we had to prepare the place. In one room the desks were all raised on bricks and the work-bench tops were clamped on them; the wooden mallets, the boxes of carving tools, each with its user's name, were lifted down from a cupboard top and properly distributed. In another room, drawing boards, T-squares, set squares, compasses, rulers, pencils and rubbers were laid out. In a third room on Tuesdays, the boxes were piled up to form a base for the lantern which the Gaffer then set up and adjusted.

Monday evening began with drawing, mainly mechanical drawing, followed by an hour's woodcarving. Tuesday evening began with woodcarving and ended with geography. The monitors were at everybody's service, but even so I almost managed to keep up with the course. The drawing was a cinch; in woodcarving I reckoned to complete five or six of the six or seven exercises undertaken during the session. The Gaffer was a very competent carver: it was he who carved the frame holding the Roll of Honour in the church porch. Carving was a joy, the more so when I graduated from whitewood and pitchpine to oak and satin walnut. The only drawback was my monitorial duty: the delicate tip-tap with the mallet on the gouge demanded utter concentration, and this was frequently broken by shouts for new wood or for a No. 5 or a V-tool to be resharpened.

The ladies left early on Tuesdays: geography was lantern slides, and blown-up pictures of Zulu chiefs with bloated bellies were not considered suitable for feminine eyes. Here discipline was lighter, though audible comment on the anatomy of naked African girls was not encouraged. Sometimes the slides didn't arrive until Tuesday and Mansey would only be able to take a quick preliminary glance, but he was never stumped. This was my first introduction to dead-pan – a racy commentary in that solemn voice with its oxymoron of gritty smoothness, rather like a bass nutmeg grater heavily muted. Occasionally, there would be a loud explosion of laughter when a particularly outlandish picture appeared on the screen, and that now beloved ho-ho-ho would rise above the rest. Even now I can almost smell that brass-and-boxwood, smoky oil lantern; even now I call projectors, 'lanterns', and receive that odd glance which an American gave me when I said I had heard a news item on my wireless telegraphy set! Incidentally, I still use the term Nightschool, that honourable word.

Afterwards, two tired boys put everything away most carefully, unclamped the bench tops, removed the bricks from the desks and toddled home at 10.30 p.m. I used to sleep with the sound of mallets in my ears and dream, occasionally, of carved patterns slowly emerging on figured oak. Years afterwards I realised that others had felt that way when the old world of learning was born anew: Chrysoloras of Byzantium was to the Gaffer as Leonardo Bruni was to me – 'I gave myself to his teaching with such ardour that my dreams at night were filled with what I had learned from him by day'.

I cannot remember exactly when the momentous decision was made; perhaps it was six or eight months after I first came to the National School, probably a little later. I was called into our front sittingroom and was surprised to find Mansey there and my parents looking rather solemn. He said he had been asking them if they would let me be a teacher, and what did I think. I said, "Would I be any good at it?" He replied, "If I didn't think so, laddie, I wouldn't be here." I said "Yes," just like that, and Dad looked a little sad. He wanted me to follow him and be a butcher or farmer, or both. I knew I couldn't possibly be a butcher – I didn't like the smell – and farming was rather a damp job. But once the decision was made, my desire grew, and Mansey saw to it that it did.

The trouble was my age – I was that late developer recorded elsewhere in this book. It was too late for a Junior County Scholarship, more or less the equivalent of Eleven Plus, but the Somerset Education Committee offered twenty to thirty Teacher Candidate Scholarships to be taken at the age of thirteen. They provided grammar school fees, a clothing and book allowance and a bit more than that towards maintenance. Mansey undertook to coach me and would hear nothing about fees. And coach me he did, carefully and patiently, day after day, month after month. He was especially insistent on formal grammar, and for this I am profoundly grateful: only those who are grounded in grammar are properly equipped and licensed to mutilate the English language. The one thing he couldn't teach me was History. "It's no good", he said, "I don't know any"; so he lent me the history textbook he had used at college, ordered me to fend for myself, and then thrilled me with stories of local history in his own native New Forest. Out came the pencil; a neat map was drawn, and soon I knew exactly which way William Rufus travelled to his death, and the route by which the unfortunate Walter Tyrrel escaped.

I got that scholarship. My parents were proud enough, but the Gaffer nearly did his nut; it was only the second open award the school had gained and the first of such (minor) financial magnitude. He boasted openly about it, but never did he take one mite of credit to himself. But I knew the truth, even then.

We left at the same time, he at the age of about fifty-one to go to a larger headship, I, at thirteen plus, to my grammar school and the road to usherdom along which he had destined me. We kept happily in touch during the few years which remained. He came to Congregation to see me take my degree; six months later he was dead, suddenly. When I went to the funeral, his widow told me he had said that when he died I was to have the massive Times Atlas he had recently acquired, the magic carpet he rode to Samarkand and Cotopaxi, the sword by which he held the gorgeous East in fee.

He gave me the basis for future standards. I have only to think of him, and other men, the power fiends, the manipulators of an acquisitive society, become distasteful. Painters, sculptors, poets, dramatists, masters of prose, composers – these stand next to the angels. Then come doctors, nurses, vets, dentists and teachers; if you feel that way you can shove in philosophers and priests at this point, though I think that they, poor chaps, are for ever batting on a drying wicket. After that, long after that, come the rest of mankind. To heal and to teach – those are the jobs; and I have never met anyone who could teach better than Hugh Mansey, my old Gaffer.

Chapter Eleven

WAR IN THE VILLAGE

Like the late George Bernard Shaw, I don't care nowadays for birthday celebrations. Long ago, it was different: my twenty-first party was such a success that we had another like it a year later.

In 1968 I had my sixty-third birthday, the termination of my grand climacteric and time for reflection on many things. I realised that I belonged to the youngest living group of those who span the chasm – who could really remember what things were like before 4th August 1914. In another twenty years, there will only be a few thousands who remember, in another twenty-five, a handful of quavering old crones and gaffers, near centenarians, will be alone by the fireside of fading memory.

But that lovely summer day of August 3rd, that golden evening of civilised life, is vividly in my mind. During the previous year or so, the charabanc had made its impact on our village life, and particularly on my father. Right from the moment that the internal combustion engine became reasonably reliable, he loved a ride in a motor car or charabanc, and so did I. Neither of us was interested in how the things worked; neither of us had the slightest desire to drive a car; neither of us was ever specially interested in cars as quick means of getting from one place to another, but we both loved a nice ride. Just before the First War, and, again, just afterwards, my father was an inveterate organiser of charabanc parties. His enormous nose would sniff the early morning air, and he would say, "Going to be a spell of fine weather; time we had another charabanc outing." We were on one of those outings on that August 3rd, 1914, but I cannot remember if he had arranged it – I don't think so: there were rather too many non-family there. It was a stupendous day for a small boy – Exmoor, Dartmoor, Dawlish, Teignmouth and Torquay, all for the first time, all in one day. Never before so much heather, so much bracken, so many rolling, purple hills, so many white Mediterranean houses standing up against such a deep blue sea. Even the grown-ups almost forgot the war clouds until we stopped at Taunton on the homeward journey. Then the young men heard the cries of the newsboys, scrambled out of the charabanc and shouted excitedly over the news. The next morning, my father came into my bedroom and woke me. "We are at war with Germany, son", he said.

"Will you have to go and fight?" I asked.

"No, no. I'm a bit too old and it will soon be all over."

Yes, of course, it would soon be all over. I knew all about war. There were those glamorous cigarette cards, 'Regimental Uniforms', and all the others, so I knew about the traditions of our invincible regiments; indeed, there was a framed Cohen Weenen 'General' – a youthful-looking Sir John French – perched on a little bracket over the sideboard. There was my book about soldiers which Uncle John Crease had given me last Christmas. There was ex-Colour-Sergeant Baber along Claverham Road – grey but erect, fierce in appearance, gentle in voice. There was old Major Atkins, with his Inverness cape, bowed body and large, solitaire ring; his battles had been over long before the Boer War. Yes, there was the Boer War; I had played that game many a time while my elders were talking at the dining table. "Some more meat, son?"

"No thanks, Dad".

"Some more runner beans?"

"No thanks, Mother". Potatoes and gravy were the thing; mash 'em all up and then carve out the ridges, copjes and ravines of the Transvaal. There were the Boers right at the far rim of the plate. "Dismount! Quiet! Lead your horses and keep under cover! We must be nearly behind their guns now." Pull the fork slowly, round, round, round. 'Now, quick, mount! CHARGE!' A rapid splatter with knife and fork. "What a mess you are making, boy. Eat up your potato, it's all getting cold." That was the way to beat the Germans – no wicked dum-dum bullets.

Half a dozen of the best young horsemen in the village suddenly disappeared: the North Somerset Yeomanry was going to war. King Albert became a hero. The Kaiser had a withered arm and, possibly, a club foot. You did funny things with the alphabet and the Beast in the Book of Revelation and the result spelt 'Kaiser' (Earlier it had been made to spell 'Napoleon'; later, it was to spell 'Hitler'). I learnt a jingle from other boys–

> 'Kaiser Bill
> Took a pill
> Up on Cadbury Hill . . . . '

The rest is not printable; it included a most curious dialect verb and disastrous results to the Kaiser's shirt. There was an air of exhilaration among the older people, and this was intensified after the first recruiting meeting on the village green – Brave Little Belgium; Your Duty; A Just Cause – but I noticed that grand old man, Tommy Gurnett, the signalman, and his wife walking down the church causeway after the meeting. They were hand-in-hand (something only very young lovers did in those days) and they were weeping when everyone else had been cheering. Their two youngest boys, the only ones still at home, had been in the rush of those who had stepped forward and almost overwhelmed the recruiting officer. I cannot remember another recruiting meeting like it – all the best lads of military age went early in that war, and a good many did not come back again.

Then the news became bad. The Belgians were overwhelmed; Mons was fought; the Angel legend came to the village, and so, too, did the news of the first casualties: young Kingcott, Stuart Jackson's brother and two more were dead. Perhaps the other boys would not be back by Christmas. Even so, it was a long time before the war bit deep into village life. True, the spy scare died down fairly soon and people stopped looking askance at Mr. F. a German by birth but long naturalised, and began to take a lively interest in his forehead – he had recently

72

undergone some sort of trepanning operation. Anyhow, he was obviously a gentleman and a magistrate and nobody could imagine *him* transfixing babies with a bayonet. However, for years Aunt Fanny was convinced that Mr. and Mrs. M. were spies. She swore that the long chain which went round the woman's neck and down inside her blouse had a miniature revolver at its terminus – "When she bent down, my dear, I saw it with my own eyes." Like all the other village boys, I drew battle cruisers with flames stabbing out from enormous guns and black smoke belching from funnels. I followed the fortunes of the rival armies, moving little coloured flags on the map of Europe. I answered politely and correctly, but a little sullenly, when rich Mrs. H. questioned me on our allies, the names of their capital cities, the supposed strength of their armies and who was fighting alongside whom, and where. She died in 1915, and Mr. H. raised an enormous red granite monument, capped with an urn, over her grave; then he soon moved from the district and married his lovely, golden-haired, honey-skinned parlourmaid and, I hope, lived happily ever afterwards – I hope so, for she was kind-hearted, he was a nice man and his Sunbeam car was a delight to the eye.

Change in the village came gradually with the drain on manpower. I noticed that people who had lost their sons, or stood in danger of losing them, stopped talking about the war with bravado or indignation; indeed, they didn't talk much, unless their lads did anything which roused their pride to bursting point, as when that pillar of integrity, old Tom Gurnett, heard that one of his boys was being sent home from the trenches to train to be an officer – an *officer* AND a *gentleman*! Slowly, war became total war: that hypnotic Kitchener poster; Lord Derby's armlets; the boys who were waiting to be eighteen or big enough to pass for eighteen; finally, conscription. Then, there was hardly a home in the village which wasn't directly or indirectly involved; the war had come to stay.

For a small boy, however, it remained kaleidoscopic. There were the Belgian refugees, including that handsome, dashing boy, August van Wetter, who learnt English in less than no time, joined the Scouts, got us into scrapes and out of them, and boxed superbly. There was the blackout, sternly enforced by Langford, the village bobby, though no Zep. came within a hundred miles of the place. Later, there were the London refugees who did know about Zeppelins. With them, the language difficulty was greater than with the Belgians: Zummerzet with a Walloon or Flemish accent was easier to understand than Cockney. Aeroplanes slowly ceased to be a rarity; but when one crash-landed on a Sunday morning in the next village, there was a pilgrimage to it. Only one man and six boys sang in the choir that morning, and the vicar preached sadly on Absent Friends. There was the great day when five thousand of Kitchener's men route-marched through the village and halted for a break; and all down the mile-long street, tea, coffee, cocoa, lemonade, cider, beer and whisky lowed out of the front doors. A month or so later, nearly all the five thousand perished in France. There were the intercession services in the church; the large, perpendicular windows couldn't be blacked out, but P.C. Langford ignored the three flickering candles. We sang 'O God of Love, O King of Peace', and Vicar Wright's lovely quavering voice intoned the Intercession; and on our way out, we turned our torches to our left as we passed through the south porch to see if Hugh Mansey, the village schoolmaster, had added in neat script the latest names to the Roll of Honour – names known to us all.

Soon, our own family was involved; not deeply, for most of my generation were much too young and the others were too old. Cousin Harold Masters went into the army; he was getting on and fit only for home service, which I believe he found very dull. His brother, Wesley, joined the navy and enjoyed himself as a petty officer cook in a soft billet at Devonport – until he was posted to a destroyer. Cousin Owen Edwards joined the Somerset Light Infantry, but quickly found himself in the Inniskilling Fusiliers. He was in Gough's Fifth Army in March, 1918, and spent the rest of the war in a coal mine in the Ruhr. Here he snatched himself from the edge of starvation by making a key to the German potato store and raiding it by night. His reminiscences enthralled me; for this best beloved of my cousins, intelligent, observant, reflective, gentle and humorous, made me realise better than any book I have read what the First War meant to the ordinary soldier in France and in captivity.

Rationing came late in the war, and even then it was slowly worked out empirically in the English way – there was no previous experience, as in 1939-45. It didn't hit the countryside so heavily as the towns, but even a small village boy could see its effects – dirty grey bread instead of white; some commodities disappearing altogether; poor quality sweets; tubs of inferior broken biscuits selling like hot cakes; greater care given to garden produce; allotments for those who had little garden space of their own. Even at home we noticed the shortage of fats. I am hazy about dates, but I think my father reduced his herd of dairy cows to three near the beginning of the war, and these few soon went. Anyhow, there seemed to be only a short interval between the time we sold milk and the time we began to buy it. The old paddlechurn and the newer end-over-end churn lay idle, and we were glad to make a small amount of butter by taking it in turns to shake thin cream in a glass sweet jar.

There was always a sharp distinction in my mind between *real* soldiers and the Local Defence Volunteers, the Home Guard of the First War, in their pea-green uniforms. They were an earnest, serious lot, but all the small boys I knew regarded them with amusement. We watched them digging trenches – they just hadn't a clue. They would stand and argue for half an hour and then mark out the lines on the turf and set to work laboriously. I wanted to shout, "You fellows ought to imagine that the Huns are only a quarter of a mile off; you need my cousin, Owen, to show you how to get moving." Then we would wait for the inevitable – we knew they had chosen the wrong spot and would come on solid rock about two feet down. And what piddling little trenches they were – they weren't even good enough for us to play in. Their drilling on the school playground was even worse, but that was the fault of their commanding officer, a kind, amiable gentleman who didn't know the rudiments of it. One evening, my father and I were passing the playground and saw two uniformed figures, the schoolmaster, Hugh Mansey, and a former pupil, Dick North, standing outside, red-faced and doubled up with mirth. When they had cooled down a bit, Mr. Mansey gasped, "I've just been thrown out of my own playground." The C.O. didn't know the words of command: the whole company had found itself crushed against one stone wall and still trying to march through it, with the rear ranks busily and delightedly marking time by bumping the volunteers in front up their behinds. Hugh Mansey, who knew all drillbooks, military and educational, from A to Z, and young Dick who had been thoroughly put through it by Mansey, had committed the direst sin – they had laughed in the ranks! The next day, Mansey addressed his boys in the playground: "We are now going to do some drill and, unlike some of your fathers, we are *not* going to march through that wall." I was the worst performer: even my legs and feet were laughing. The little man trotted past me and hissed in a stage whisper, his straggly moustaches twitching with enjoyment: "Pick up your feet, lad, pick 'em up –there have been enough people thrown out of this yard lately."

Real soldiers were different. Men home on leave were heroes to me – silent heroes most of them, for they wanted to forget for a few precious days the Hell they had left behind them. Oddly enough, the normally quiet ones were willing to tell me about it. Lads like Cousin Owen were the backbone of the British Army, steadfast, reliable, willing to endure, adepts in the tenuous art of survival. He stripped the glamour from my mind and recreated the Flanders of 1917. I read it all later in Sassoon and others, but there was no bitterness in Owen's gentle, matter-of-fact narrative, punctuated now and again with laughter at the ludicrous. I learnt about trench hygiene; how to deal effectively with rats at night and tactfully with fussy officers by day; how to do a little salutary delousing (there was no remedy against bugs); how to behave on night patrol in No Man's Land; how to dodge the whirling canister from a Minniwerfer; how to pick out the different sounds of shells in a barrage and judge one's own degree of relative safety; how to respect dangerous positions covered by German snipers or machine guns; how best to use an entrenching tool to make a foxhole at speed during a limited advance; how to shave safely without a mirror. For some months he was a stretcher-bearer and quickly came to a detailed knowledge of all that war could do to human bodies – "If they are pretty bad, but not dying, they don't usually make much noise." He carried off desperately wounded men who returned whole and fit three months later; he saw a man struck in the forearm by a partially spent bullet and dead in three seconds. He had no particular enmity towards Germans and respected the German soldier – "Jerry is pretty hot on the bayonet; you need to watch your step." He made no violent criticisms of his immediate officers or of Higher Command; the nearest he ever got to it was uttered on his return from Germany – he said, "I was on rising ground before I was taken and had a good view; and I reckon we could have held them if we had been allowed to do so". His only bitter comment was on the quality and scarcity of cigarettes.

Another soldier friend, George Hillman, nearly twenty years older than myself, came from the next village. He wouldn't talk much about the fighting, but when I asked him if he was ever frightened, he said, "Lots of times, boy, but especially once." He was in the Royal Engineers, but got lost in the March retreat of 1918 and found himself in the midst of a Highland regiment. He was roped in to cook for them but on the next morning he had to run for his life – in his innocence he put sugar in the porridge! He cherished the memory of his final leave shortly before the Armistice. He turned up at the parish church for Evensong. During the last hymn, the local pork butcher came singing loudly down the aisle, with the collection bag in his hand. Suddenly he spotted George, pumped his hand vigorously and said, "My boy, I be so glad to see you safe and sound and away from them horrible trenches." Then he remembered his duty, resumed singing 'All praise and thanks to God' and relieved the next two pews of pennies and tanners. Suddenly he rushed back and shouted, "Tell your mother I've got a nice bit of bacon saved back for her." Nothing was too good for the boys.

The end seemed to come suddenly. There was no mafficking in our village on that first Armistice Day. The vicar came into the school just before the end of the morning, told us the news and wept as he said a few prayers – *his* boy was now safe. We were sent home for the rest of the day. The church bells rang joyously that evening and I believe the pubs were fairly full. Otherwise, it was quiet everywhere, very, very quiet, like a super-Sunday. My mother just said, "I hope poor dear Owen will come back safely from Germany."

Chapter Twelve

ON THE MOVE

Rustics whose memories go back beyond the First World War knew a world which in many ways had changed little since the 16th century, a world of relative immobility. When I was born, John Loudon McAdam had been dead for only sixty-nine years and Thomas Telford for seventy-one; it would have been possible for my grandfather to have known them. They and their successors and imitators gave good surfaces to roads and enabled coach-builders to make well-sprung, smooth-running vehicles; otherwise my boyhood way of getting around differed little from that of my two close friends, Sir John Petre in Elizabethan times and old Benjamin Mildmay, Earl Fitzwalter, in the first half of the 18th century. Admittedly, we had a railway station, and, even before my time, our village was beginning to be a dormitory of Bristol. There were three or four motor cars around, but these harbingers of speed were still for the few; travel for most of us was limited by the capacity of the horse.

The horse, that strange anachronism; if it weren't for the foxes, the bookies and little girls with ponytails and jodphurs, it would have been extinct a generation ago. Nowadays I cannot bestir myself to go and see any of those archaic pageants which keep the horse in existence; they are all a bit like heart transplants and drugs to keep alive those who are ancient and incurable. All the same, I wish I had bothered to learn more than two things about a horse. Perhaps, with a couple of revision lessons, I could manage to groom and harness one; perhaps I could still manage to mount one and endure, once again, the agony of that bottom-rasping, undulatory means of motion. Nothing more than that. Now Dad and Uncle Ted were different. Uncle Ted was an expert. My father was not far behind: in his last years in the 1950s, I saw him in his dressing gown pad out into the yard to examine a hunter. Although he was old, and a little tottery after recovering from six strokes, the skill was all there. Making the authentic hissing noises, he seized time by the fetlock, examined every point meticulously and delivered a trenchant judgment.

My boyhood roads were all well-made but untarred – macadamised, but not tarmac. They had serious defects. For instance, McAdam's theory was sound enough, but in practice it was impossible to ensure that all stones in the cambered surface were firmly bound together. A horse's hoofs would knock out a loose stone; others would follow; the rain would get in and the pot-hole would rapidly grow. Dry weather would produce the other main defect, dust, sometimes ankle deep. From every horse-drawn vehicle it would rise in little puffs; the occasional

77

motor-car would raise a billowing cloud, and this would settle and make the dense foliage of wayside hedgerows seem like out-of-season mayflower. Motoring veils were not confined to ladies in motor cars; my mother and Aunt Fanny, sitting in the back of our jubilee car or in the hired wagonette were glad to wear them. North Somerset seemed to be full of swathed women hurrying to take swarms of bees.

The remedy for dust was water. Nowadays, the summer shower has lost much of its joy. In the golden years of the past, one didn't run for shelter straight away: it was worth getting damp just to have the pleasure of seeing those cocoa-coloured bubbles of dusty wetness rolling into the gutter. Then, when the storm was spent, there was that delicious smell of slaked road – far, far better than the stench of petrol or diesel. Incidentally, somebody ought to write a history of smells – slaked roads, ammoniated stables, harness oil, new bread baked in a brick oven, boot blacking, beeswax and turpentine, smouldering candlewick, naphtha lamps on fairgrounds, Stockholm tar, cottagers' piggeries.

But the rain rarely came to order. Nor did the watering-cart belonging to the Rural District Council: it had an enormous area to cover; its driver must have felt he was in the Augean Stables. The real answer was the hosepipe, long enough to slake the stretch of street from Upton Villa next door, past our house, shop and yard and down to the forecourt of *The Bell*. It was a task to be done thoroughly and spun out as long as possible; sheer bliss, especially if one's pals happened to be passing on their bikes and had to run the gauntlet, though one had to be willing to suffer reprisals.

I cannot help feeling a sad pride in being a survival – one of the last generation to see some of the great village craftsmen at work. Watching the coachmakers was most rewarding. All our own vehicles were made locally. Our high, wonderfully light, smooth-running gig – black, with red-striped shafts, spokes, vellies and hubs – was skilfully constructed by cousin Walter Yeates from an old Victoria. The low-slung Jubilee car was sturdy, but light enough in weight for Kitty, the pony, to pull easily with four up. The butcher's cart, a light-weight, was made, I believe, by Walter Yeates; the van was strong and solid. The high 'putt', or cart, and the gracefully-designed waggon took care of the harder farm work. Waggons were superb examples of craftsmanship, of the way in which slow evolution to give fitness for purpose could also give aesthetic pleasure; fine examples, too, of regional characteristics to meet regional needs. Then, there was that utility vehicle, the crankaxle cart, a general run-about, highly useful to a farmer and even more so to one who was also a butcher. Stick a couple of large baskets, crammed with ribs of beef and loins of pork, in the back; deliver them to housewives, and then pick up half-a-dozen lambs from Farmer Burdge.

In my boyhood, the village street, over a mile long, was nearly always busy, a civilised busy-ness of roll-and-rattle, and tap-tap-tap. Today it is a deafening inferno and death trap, with cars and lorries roaring through from Clevedon to Weston-Super-Mare and Bristol, and vice versa.

Back in the days before 1914, the street came to life early. I was always waked by the clatter of milk-floats racing to the station to catch the early milk-train – a twenty-minute stampede, always ending with the rapid clip-clip of Percy Griffin's high-stepping cob. Then came the slower, intermittent sounds of the local milkmen delivering pints and quarts and crying out "Whoa" to their horses. These were interspersed with the smart trot of carriage or gig, bearing Bristol commuters to the station, and the bicycle bells or tramping feet of workmen going to Wake and Dean's furniture factory. During the day, there would be considerable variety – tradesmen's vehicles, farm carts, governess cars, Mr. Clements' wagonette, brake-loads of beery men pulling into *The Prince of Orange*, occasional gipsy caravans, brightly painted, the massive trunk of a noble elm, dragged by sweating shirehorses. Best of all were dog carts; I don't know why, possibly because we didn't have one and Uncle Ted did, and I adored him more than any man I've known. They were classless; anybody could own one, from stately gentlemen down to George and Johnny King, brothers, but bitter rivals as chimney sweeps. They weren't twins, but they looked alike, and it was a social gaffe to call George, "Johnny", or the other way round. Fortunately, this didn't often happen: Johnny always wore a cap and George sported an old black beaver. Come to think of it, I never saw either bareheaded; it is a good idea to keep your hat on when you sweep chimneys.

The age of horse power wasn't just a matter of horse, cart and road. Think of all the accoutrements and by-products. Not merely harness, though that was fascinating enough and justified the old adage, 'There's nothing like leather'. Think, for example, of carriage and cart lamps, lovely beautiful examples of honest craftsmanship. Even today, their romantic appeal has survived. I am never tired of airing my dislike of revivalism in all its forms, but I cannot get beyond a tolerant smile of pity for those whose smart villas have their front doors flanked by a pair of carriage lamps, lit, of course, by electricity. There is even a flourishing trade, I'm told, in counterfeiting them for that purpose. But I am old enough to know the real pleasure of real carriage lamps, derived from tending them, cleaning them, trimming them. They have conditioned my attitude to illumination. I am a little vague on volts, amps and watt-nots, and feel happiest at those rare moments when another old codger tells me that his powerful torch is equivalent to so-much candle power!

For long-distance travel, steam was king when I was young. Yatton station was proud and important. It stood on one of the longest straight stretches of the G.W.R. and the expresses which thundered through used to frighten me when I was very small. But all other trains, even 'fast' ones, stopped there, and its own pride was echoed by the porters crying out, "Yatton. Change for the Clevedon, Cheddar Valley and Wrington Vale lines". Alas, the Wrington Vale went long ago; Lord Beeching (or his successor) closed the Cheddar Valley; the little motor-train service to Clevedon is dead and gone; and, now, more and more road traffic hurtles through the village street. No more of those cheap circular tickets – along the Wrington Vale; alight at Burrington; climb the famous Combe, past The Rock of Ages and Aveline's Hole; branch off to the right and follow the little stream upwards through bracken more than head high. Then, strike across the heather on the east flank of Blackdown, 1,068 feet up; past the little Roman amphitheatre; move over to Charterhouse; drop down the grass-covered lead workings of Velvet Bottom; then, down the great Cheddar Gorge, a mile and a half long, and more awesome at every step. Then catch the seven-something train at Cheddar and come home by the Cheddar Valley line.

Railwaymen were proud, confident men when I was young. They served the G.W.R., the best railway company in the world; Yatton railwaymen served a

79

proud junction. They worked long hours and were not well paid, but they had position and commanded respect. They did their job well and had no use for scrimshankers. They ran the trains to time, without having a Mussolini to bully them; and if a train were delayed by mishap or inclement weather, they felt personally and collectively responsible for letting the public down. The goods' service was reliable; the passenger trains were clean, and those beautiful green engines, with their gleaming brass and copper, were lovingly groomed and serviced. And do you remember those breakfasts served by the G.W.R. restaurant cars forty or fifty years ago?

Steam on the road was not to be missed. Long before the great lumbering traction-engine came round the bend by the Butcher's Arms, two hundred yards down the street, the windows would begin to shake and I would dash to the end wall of the yard and watch its approach. In those quiet days, noise was a novelty. It rattled, it rumbled, it clanked and clattered, it hissed and belched smoke and sparks – it was just like Satan with stomach-ache. Steam rollers were nearly as good. Better still were the engines which bore the paraphernalia of fairs and circuses; painted, gleaming and romantic. Besides, with circuses, one could hear the muffled roar of a poor boxed-up lion or see the measured tread of the elephants, just like Mr. George Needham, the undertaker.

Steam-power drove Dr. Peter Johnson's car. It was the first automobile in the village, but, about the time I was born, Frankie Lyons, who lived next door, acquired the village's first, real, petrol-powered motor. He was an amateur, who bought the car for his own pleasure, but he wasn't above hiring out himself and it to his acquaintances. It wasn't very reliable – occasionally we had to get out and shove behind. Dad would eye the car sardonically: he would say, 'Come on, push hard! I've never had to push the backside of a horse'. By contrast, my father's buddy, Wally Coward, who had set up the first garage in the neighbourhood, at Congresbury, the next village, could always be relied on to get us there and back again. Then, Albert Bird ('Dicky-Bird'), who had spent many years in the States and still spoke with an American accent, bought one of the very first T-model Fords. When Dad hired it, I was usually allowed to sit beside Dicky Bird and watch the speedometer needle slowly rise to a reckless forty-five m.p.h. as he moved the throttle lever on the steering-wheel.

Young boys, like ordinary adult mortals, didn't have cars; they rode bicycles and dreamed of the day when they would own a powerful, dashing Red Indian motor-bike. Even in those days there were status symbols. I began as the lowest of the low: my first bike was a second-hand fix-wheel; tiring to ride and rather boring – one had to keep pedalling on and on, although brief respite could be gained going downhill by putting one's feet on either side of the front fork. Next up the social scale were ordinary free-wheelers and free-wheelers with backpedalling brakes. Boys with two-speed or three-speed models were vastly envied. Even in this range, there were gradations in status. Inferior people had a V-shaped piece of metal, with a little lever, fixed to the top bar of the frame, and a naked wire ran along the top bar and down to the hub; superior folk had a plated, flick-over job fixed to the handlebars and the wire was fully-clothed. Well-to-do adults bought the best bikes; not Raleighs – they were rising rapidly but were not yet kings of the road. One of the two best machines was the Sunbearm, the Rolls-Royce of cycles. The other has a double-barrelled name which I forget. It was a strange contraption with a high unusual frame and a string saddle. It was becoming outmoded by the Sunbeam, but was still much favoured by military-looking gents in Norfolk jackets and plus fours, or, rather, plus one-and-three-quarters. These old boys mounted their steel steeds *via* the back step, a curious heaving, wobbling procedure, looking to my rude little bucolic eyes rather like an astigmatic bull going into action.

My first cycle lamp was appropriate to my lowly fix-wheel status – a miserable, messy little oil lamp which tended to go out when one bumped over a pot-hole. Not that lamplight was essential to safety in those days, except, perhaps in a night fog – one knew the roads well and there were few hot-toed motorists; lamps were needed mainly because the law said so. But how I longed to possess one of those superb, waspwaisted Lucas carbide lamps, with the cut emerald on one side and the cut ruby on the other and its long clear range of illumination. A few years ago, I was at Church Farm, Stebbing, looking at Frank Howland's collection of old vehicles and other byegones, including one of those early Douglas motorbikes. I turned to that most genial and hospitable of Essex farmers and mentioned my boyhood ambition. "Like this?", said Frank, reaching up to a shelf and bringing down a perfect specimen. Incidentally, I then said, "I'll stump you, now, Frank. Bet you haven't got one of those old lemonade bottles with the glass marble stopper". "Haven't I, boy", replied Frank, whisking one from behind me. He bent down, rummaged in a box, and then said, "And here's another". How pleasant it was to visit that lovely Essex farm only a few miles away and become a Somerset boy once again.

How old was I when I saw my first aeroplane? Four, or five, perhaps – I'm too lazy to look up the records. Anyhow, it was one of those early, round-England races by a Frenchman, a German and an Englishman, named, I believe, Valentine. The villagers declared that the winner, the Frenchman, passed over in the night; Fred Baber, prince of spoofers, swore that the knife he had picked up on Cadbury Hill had been dropped by it. Early next morning, my mother snatched me from bed, ran downstairs, dropped me, picked me up and ran out into the street in time for me to see that kite-like affair of Valentine's slowly moving across, the north west horizon. I was cross – my bottom and my dignity had been hurt by the bumping I had received. On the whole, aeroplanes have continued to make me cross. Admittedly, I was thrilled and grateful when for weeks on end I had a grandstand view of the northern half of the Battle of Britain, and especially so when Bader chased a Messerschmidt 109 across the sky and shot it down.

Chapter Thirteen

PORTBRIDGE MILL

A letter from Aunt Louie was an event, for it nearly always meant an invitation to Portbridge Mill. It had probably been fished for: my father was an inveterate visitor. Not that we weren't welcome – it was quite accepted among my father's generation that any one of them would suddenly express a desire to descend upon another. It was always a joy to see a letter from one of Dad's sisters; it was rarely given to me, a mere child, to read, but I could see the characteristic handwriting across the breakfast table. All three sisters wrote alike in that tall but far from angular hand common to all girls who had gone to school in mid-Victorian times. Besides, I knew it would have the family peculiarities – a liberal sprinkling of inverted commas which they invariably called 'brackets' and used for emphasis rather than 'quotes'; direct speech was denoted by heavy underlining.

Portbridge Mill was on the boundary between Chew Magna and Chew Stoke, only about ten miles from home, but getting there was a major undertaking. There were six of us: my father and mother, Aunt Fanny, Dad's unmarried sister, Cousin Arthur (now my brother-in-law) my sister and myself. Our gig, drawn by Paddy (and, later, by Doctor) would only hold three; the low-slung Jubilee car would hold us all, but the steep pull up Brockley Combe would be too much for Kitty the pony; so my father used to hire Mr. Clement's wagonette – two in front and two facing two behind. Even so, the journey would take well over the hour, most of it in the mile-long climb up Brockley Combe, with one or two of us getting off, walking behind and giving a shove to help old Paddy along. Not that this slow progress mattered, for I always loved the sombre beauty of the Combe; the steep, winding road, the massive beeches with hearts and initials carved on their trunks, the clean, limestone rocks seen towering above through gaps in the green tunnel of trees, the moss-grown boulders and cliffs under the trees, one of them split by a yew from which some distracted young woman hanged herself by her stockings. When I was about eleven, dear old Mansey, the village schoolmaster, made us learn Coleridge's poem on the Combe, certainly not one of the poet's better efforts. It began–

> 'With many a pause and oft reverted eye
> I climb the Combe's ascent: sweet songsters near
> Warble in shade their wild wood melody . . . '

Its ending always moved me to ribald laughter:

'Deep sighs my lonely heart: I drop the tear:
Enchanting spot! O were my Sara here.'

The middle stretch of the journey was always a bit boring, but as we dropped gently down towards Winford, I began to perk up. We always watched to catch a glimpse of Aunt Louie's elder son, Harold Masters, and his family as we passed his house in Winford Street. Sometimes we would stop there for a few minutes, though never long enough for my liking. He was a wheelwright, though, later, when the craft of wheelwrighting was overwrought, he became an engineer in the Redding Works nearby. His workshop and yard seemed a paradise to a small boy: there was the violent hiss and pungent smell as a red-hot bonded wheel was plunged in the pool; there was the gorgeous smell of paint as Harold's skilled and steady brush marked in the black lines on the red background of spokes and vellies.

The Redding works, as we called them, meant that Portbridge Mill was very near. Nobody ever explained to me what they were really *for;* I still don't even know how they were *spelt* – I see they are just called 'Colour Mills' on the Ordnance Survey Map. But they were certainly *red*: every building was covered by a red deposit, and so, too, were the men who worked there – redder than the Red Indians in books. I think the raw material which went into the works was clay containing red oxide of lead, which was extracted there; but I have never troubled to find out about it.

At the cross-roads beyond the Redding works we turned left and moved down the slope to the stream on which both the works and Portbridge Mill stood. The gate to the mill, shaded by an enormous walnut tree, was right beside the bow bridge where the road crossed the stream. The short drive to the house and mill was flanked on the left by ash trees, and their leaves brushed our hats as the wagonette rolled slowly by.

Uncle William Masters would come out to greet us as the wagonette drew up in front of the house. In the years around the First World War he was in his sixties. He was fairly tall, balding, with a grizzled ginger moustache and side whiskers and a high complexion. He was always kind to me, but I was a little scared of him: he had a gruff voice, a rather austere and authoritarian manner, and, unlike all the Edwards family, he didn't talk much. He was the only one of my older near relatives who had gone to a grammar school. I thought he was wise and godlike, whereas, I know now that he was neither. Aunt Louie was my father's eldest sister, some eighteen years his senior: she was shortish, fairly plump and rosy cheeked. She was vivacious, talked with a high- pitched voice and had a nervous falsetto laugh. Gertie, their daughter, was only about a couple of years younger than my mother. She was tall, thin, straight as a poplar. She had an aquiline nose, high cheekbones and a red complexion – I always thought she looked like a Red Indianess, but was too polite to say so. Her voice was pretty near an octave higher than Aunt Louie's. She always treated me with a brisk, brusque, bustling kindness, just as if she were trying to hustle a hen and chickens back into their coop. Wesley Arthur, alias Jack, the younger son, much younger than Gertie and Harold, was always something of an irrepressible schoolboy, but he had that rare and precious knack of invoking affection and holding it.

The whole place was a sheer joy to a small boy. The house and mill formed one building, three storeys high and built probably in the early 19th century. Attached to the mill at right angles was a two-storeyed bakery and store for ground corn. In the angle of the L was a square patch of cobblestones, partly covered by a large porch. Here, Uncle William would sit on a heavy wooden bench and smoke his vile pipe; I never knew his brand of tobacco, but it smelt like a mixture of dung and gunpowder.

It was a wonderful place for smells: the acrid smell of stale tobacco throughout the house (they rarely opened a window); the oxymoron of the mill – the sweet smell of freshly ground corn, laced with the sour whiff of rat and mouse; the smell of dough in the white scrubbed kneading troughs; the magnificent scent of newly baked bread coming out of the brick oven on the scorched blades of the long peels. Even the earth-closet had a unique aroma and a unique and fascinating design. As a little rustic who already had vast experience of eccentric rural closets, including two-deckers and three-holers, I always visited it with awe. It was the only closet I knew where one had to mount steps to enter. Inside, was a well-scrubbed deal throne, a comely and competent piece of carpentry. I think it must have been made by Cousin Harold. I never saw much of him and never knew him well, but he had that odd, creative quality which I used to notice in several of the Edwards gang – the gift of being able to materialize a fantasy. When he was a lad, long before my time, he was responsible for the contents of a bottle which used to stand on the mantelpiece in Aunt Fanny's bedroom; not the usual ship, but a rather terrifying raguly cross, ringed by a collection of tools, including a ladder, a pickaxe and a shovel; it may have been a survival, in a debased and unknowing form, of the Emblems of the Passion. I used to spend ages looking at it; and in later years I've always had a kindly, sympathetic feeling towards George III who couldn't understand how the apple got inside the dumpling.

Away to the south of the house, towards the paddock and orchard, stretched the outbuildings. There were henhouses, the dog's kennel, a very piggy piggery, the wash-house, the stables and oxhouse. Against the dwellinghouse itself was a coachhouse-*cum*-harness-room, with its rich composite odour of harness oil, Brasso and lamp candle. It sheltered the coburg, the two-wheeled van for delivering the bread – that wonderful, crisp bread with chestnut-coloured crust. In the south of England few people under fifty now know what bread is: every day, millions of ignorant creatures chew away contentedly at their insipid cotton wool, without the least twinge of nostalgia. "Hey, boy, take this," Uncle William Masters would cry, breaking off the top knob of a cottage loaf fresh and warm from the brick oven. I would run in to Aunt Louie; she would open up the knob, slap a big wedge of butter inside, close it up again and hand it back. The thing to do was to wait for a few minutes before eating; the melting butter would then have seeped outwards towards the crust. Ambrosia couldn't possibly taste better.

There was a narrow little cinder path which led from the yard, round the back of the main building to the closet with the throne. Then one went through a door of the back kitchen, out through another and down some stone steps to a square, brick-lined well or catchment, where the water from a tiny fern-lined spring was held before flowing under the house to the main stream. This was the household water supply. It was always crystal clear and icy cold even in the hottest summer, but, somehow, I was a little suspicious of it. I think this was because, rather unusually in the countryside, I had been used to piped water from very early childhood. In our village, a neat little waterworks pumped the water from a Domesday well to a reservoir high up in Henley Wood so that it could flow down again at high pressure to supply the village. It would spout angrily from the tap, and it was so full of minute air bubbles that it looked like translucent milk. I loved to watch the water in the glass jug clearing from the bottom upwards as the air bubbles rose. The Portbridge Mill water was probably just as good as ours, but Aunt Fanny had told me so many old wives' tales of the dangers run by small boys who drank scout-wise from streams that I poured out my fears to Aunt Louie and Cousin Gertie. They told me solemnly that all water was put through a filter in the store cupboard before it was used for drinking; but I was never allowed to look in this cupboard and they would never let me see this mythical filter. I was a gullible, trusting little boy.

A short path from the water supply led up a bank to the 'mill pond'. Then a plank bridge crossed the 'race', such as it was, to a path across the top of the weir. Strictly speaking, there was neither mill-pond nor race. The mill stood directly on the stream at a point where there was a natural drop, and all the original builder of the mill had to do was to make a weir across the waterfall. When the hatches were down, the waters upstream rose to make a 'mill pond' and their force was sufficient to drive the water wheel. When the mill was not working, the hatches were raised, the waters roared and plunged to a prodigious depth of quite ten feet! I loved to watch it; it was my first waterfall and I wouldn't have swapped it for Niagara, Victoria or the Yosemite Valley.

Below the fall, the waters rushed along the side of Gertie's flower garden, with its sweet briar and periwinkles, and flowed under the old bow bridge beside the entrance gate to mill and house. Against the parapet there was a cast-iron sign about two feet high and painted white with black lettering. This marked the boundary between the parishes of Chew Stoke and Chew Magna. I never failed to follow the usual, pleasing ritual: first, I would stand facing the sign, with legs wide apart, so that my left foot was in Chew Stoke and my right in Chew Magna; then, turn about and *vice versa*. Then I would gaze over the parapet and watch the trout in the stream, looking anxiously for the three-pounder which always eluded Cousin Wesley and all the other anglers.

Downstream, the dappled waters rippled over smooth pebbles and through a tunnel of willows, a good, safe place for paddling and catching minnows and sticklebacks. Here one could generally reckon on seeing a blue streak of light as a kingfisher flashed by. Another hundred yards or so and the stream flowed into a little lake which was a reservoir. This was always out of bounds: little boys could easily be sucked down to their death in its sedgy fringes – or so the grown-ups said!

I always prayed for fine weather when we were visiting Portbridge Mill. All the fun there was out of doors; the house was a bit poky for a family of four, plus visitors, and it reeked of Uncle William's foul tobacco; it was nothing like so fascinating as Aunt Clara's house in Bath, all neat and shiny and smelling of furniture polish. There were only two proper rooms downstairs – the kitchen-living room, which always seemed full of bustling women, and the parlour which was a Victorian museum. Apart from the primulas and maidenhair ferns in the window, the parlour repelled me – I never liked being in it alone: horsehair sofa and chairs, antimacassars everywhere, a green chenille cloth with bobbles on the table, tinkling chandeliers on the vases and glass cases crammed with stuffed birds and animals shot by the menfolk. There were even stuffed kingfishers – *kingfishers*, the epitome of light and life and flashing speed. Perhaps these cases helped to put me off killing things; in fact, the only living things I've ever shot are rats, though I have often thought the world would be a better place if I were commissioned to shoot nearly all politicians and some lawyers.

Every visit always ended with a ritual. Just inside the mill was the weighing machine for the sacks of flour. One by one, we would solemnly step on the platform, while Uncle William would lift the iron weights up and down. Then our own weights would be pencilled on the wall next to the record of our previous visit. Nobody dieted in those days: *plus* meant health, *minus* was a matter of concern to us – to 'go into a decline' was a death worse than fate. My father was a spare man until he reached his late 70s; if Uncle William's scales showed that he was a couple of pounds down on last time, he would have pains in his tummy for the next day or so and would imagine he had a 'growth'! Actually, he died very peacefully of old age in 1954 after he had completely recovered from half a dozen strokes spread out over the last twenty years of his life.

The return journey was always fairly brisk for those days – there was more *downhill* going home. Unless it was near full moon and the sky was clear, we usually set out before nightfall. Aunt Louie would pop a small pot of raspberry jam in my pocket as I climbed into the back of the wagonette. The heavy rug would be spread over our knees. It had thick, waterproofed rubber on the outside and a warm, fluffy underside striped in a tiger fashion. I would always feel hopefully to find if the shining metal hanging ring was near my corner – I liked to cling to it and turn it round and round on its swivel. If it were raining, the green carriage umbrella was opened up and Mother and Aunt Fanny would take it in turns to hold the handle with its deep yellow pineapple knob. The strong ribs and stout cover had a wide span and gave ample shelter to the four of us in the back. Before we dropped down into Brockley Combe, the carriage lights were lit. Their pale gleam picked out the edges of the winding road through the cavern of black and cast a distorted shadow of Paddy on the trunks of the huge beeches. I used to watch the little red circle of glass at the back of the offside lamp and wait until the lamp had warmed up so that I could smell the candle smoke. When we emerged at the bottom of the Combe, there was no longer any need for Dad to be a vigilant driver – old Paddy knew every bend and curve of the last three miles. He would snort and pick up his pace – home meant supper and bed for him, too.

Chapter Fourteen

BATH

There is not much point in being sorry for Bath; she can stand up to infinite badgering and still remain, as always, an enigma. For centuries the writers, famous and otherwise, have been analysing her and using up the adjectives at a prodigal rate – Pepys, Lady Mary Wortley Montagu, Smollett, Fielding, Mrs. Thrale, Harrison Ainsworth, H.A. Vachell, *et al.* Even Mr. Pickwick had his say, though Dickens got Milsom Street terribly muddled with Park Street, Bristol. Many writers see only the facet they wish to see. Arthur Waugh, not the greatest but perhaps the wisest of that literary family, called her 'A city of the 18th century, bland and beautiful, dreaming with her grey stone eyes of the glory of an unforgettable past'. Not a bad, high falutin' sentence and true; but it is only a bit of the truth. In recent years I have had to be satisfied with a brief glance, four times a year, from the train; but about ten years ago, with something of Walter Ison in my mind and Nikolaus Pevsner's North Somerset in my hand, I wandered happily around a bustling, busy city – certainly not dreaming on that day – and was surprised and delighted to find a good deal surviving that was pre-Wood and belonged to the late 17th and very early 18th century. Indeed, I am inclined to believe that the loveliest period in domestic building is the short span around 1700 – William-without-Mary; they hadn't yet learned to be self-important and over-refined.

But architectural vanity was not one of my boyhood vices. To me Bath meant an August holiday with Uncle Tom Coombe and Aunt Clara, fairly often as a small boy, regularly in my secondary school and university days, when bedroom accommodation was more readily available.

The Coombes were a remarkable family – godly, good, kind, active, contented and entirely without that envy and grasping ambition which corrode the spirit more rapidly than any other sin, deadly, or otherwise. They all had what Dr. Johnson called 'a bottom of sense'. I owe much to them; they were very fond of me and more than specially kind.

Uncle Tom was one of the few entirely good men I have ever liked or respected – I've always been firmly on the side of the sinners! He was also one of the quietest and, outwardly, one of the mildest of men; he suffered Aunt Clara to bustle him around on minor matters, but on all important issues he was the master of the household, almost the patriarch. He was of average height for his time, with fair silky hair, mutton chop whiskers, bushy moustache and mild blue eyes which could suddenly flash and become piercing if a matter of principle was involved. He rarely pushed himself, but I noticed, quite early on, that whenever he spoke, either in his household or, rarely, in public, other people listened; and when he had spoken in that quiet voice there really wasn't much that anybody else could find worth saying. In later life I have heard that kind of talk from eminent men in the corridors of minor power, but Uncle Tom was never more than the highly trusted foreman of a flour mill, which he served for the best part of sixty years.

Aunt Clara was an Edwards. This was something she could never entirely muzzle or suppress; she could be grande dame to perfection, and then, suddenly, the little imp in her would stir and out would come a devastatingly, well-salted sentence. She was a little on the short side, slim except in her later years, and her back was as straight as a guardsman. She was a proud housewife, a fine cook and a perfect manager – essential qualities in bringing up a family on a very limited income. I realised this when quite young; it was fascinating to watch her dealing with tradesmen at the door or in their shops – they regarded her with an infinite respect amounting almost to awe. It is a safe bet that she was never overcharged by a ha'penny or short-weighted by an ounce. She saw to it that the food which came into the house was worthy of the cooking she accorded it. She also had another Edwards characteristic – a will like a rapier, strong but flexible; it will bend against superior force but will not snap; and it will spring back pretty sharply. I knew the signs as a small boy; she understood that children could be awkward and not much notice should be taken of this; but when she dropped (not raised) her voice and spoke with particular politeness, I knew it was time to shut up.

My four Coombe cousins were born between 1887 and 1897; there were two others who died in infancy. Amy, the eldest, was senior mistress in a girls' elementary school; in middle age she married a Methodist minister. She was shortish, dainty in appearance and a dazzling blonde, almost white. Like her father, she was the personification of goodness: kind, just, deeply religious, cool and serene of mind, incisive in manner and speech, well aware of the wickedness in this world but never censorious. Of all the multitude of cousins on my father's side she was the least Edwards-like.

As a small boy, I adored Olive, the second eldest. She had more Edwards in her than the others, and, a natural corollary, more of Somerset in her voice. She had darkish brown hair, was about average in height and was pale in complexion. She was gay, brisk, warm-hearted, sensible and utterly independent in spirit. She remained on deeply affectionate terms with all her family, but, even as a boy, I suspected that she found the nonconformist conscience a bit too much of a good thing; anyhow, she left home as a girl to work for Lance & Lance, the drapers in Weston-Super-Mare. We were then her nearest kinsfolk, and she would frequently spend the week-end with us, though it should be noted that the week-end in those days lasted only from Saturday evening to the first train on Monday morning. I would firmly refuse to have my bath on Saturday nights until she arrived to give it to me, but I honestly cannot remember if this was on account of affection for her or a desire to postpone bedtime. When she was about thirty she married Jack Stow, a quiet, gentle Wiltshire widower with a young boy, and they then quickly produced a family of four. When she died a few years ago, I realised with regret that I hadn't seen her for thirty to forty years. Whenever I went into the west country, we always seemed to miss meeting one another by a day or so; my mother, for instance, would say, "I do wish you had been here last week; dear Olive came to see us on Thursday." But we did correspond at long intervals and never found any difficulty in picking up the threads. All the same, I feel remorse: the town of Swindon has never exercised its magnetic magic on me, but I ought to have made the effort to go there.

Ena, the youngest, was lovely: tall, slender, handsome, elegant, witty, full of fun, highly literate, highly prescient. She had an attractive speaking voice and a pleasant, well-trained, contralto singing voice. It must be the best part of fifteen years ago that she died tragically, but even after that lapse of time I cannot bring myself to write more about her.

Win, the third girl, is deliberately left to last. She was the last of the four to die and the one who was deepest in my affection. She never married. She was engaged for a time before the first World War: but a later admirer, the young officer she would probably have married, was one of the thousands who never came back from Flanders. She was a most attractive girl – vibrant, warm-hearted, even warm-tempered. She showered her affection on me as a small boy, twelve years her junior, and for long afterwards; and looking back over the years I realise I must have sorely tried her patience. We were diametrically opposite in so many ways: she was a Christian, I was always something of a sceptic; she was a Wesleyan, I was an Anglican; she had strong views on strong drink, so had I, but they weren't the same. She was a firm Liberal. As a little Tory boy I thought the Liberals were awful; now, I look on them as odd, but harmless, archaeological survivals. She thought the world could be made better by goodness and progress; I am all for leaving people alone. Of course, these differences were never sharply defined when I was small, but neither then nor afterwards, did they diminish our mutual affection. She was indomitable in giving me happiness; for instance, when I was cricket-mad she sat with me throughout a boiling day, watching Somerset and Jack White, and when I turned and looked at her at close of play the skin around her neck (she was nearly as fair as Amy) was a mass of blisters – and she hadn't made a murmur. She had all the goodness of the Coombe family and some of the less infuriating of the Edwards qualities, notably, a zest for living and a quick recognition of pomposity in others. On the penultimate time I met her – the day of my father's funeral in 1954 – she was just the same, the complete ally, instinctively on my side to protect my mother from being distressed by maudlin dirges proffered by other kinsfolk.

No. 30, Winchester Road, Oldfield Park, Bath, was easily my favourite house throughout boyhood; and, today, I am not at all sure that modern designers have planned a better type of dwelling for ordinary people with not much money. It was about halfway down a sloping terrace block built around the turn of the century – most of the family, then elsewhere in Bath, could remember when the Oldfield Park area was nearly all fields. It was three rooms up and three-and-a-half down. There was a pocket handkerchief of a garden in front, looked after by the cousins – the larger back garden was Uncle Tom's domain. The front door was solid wood and always kept open when the family was at home. About three feet inside it was a second door, full of multicoloured glass, through which the sun would cast mottled hues of distorted shapes on the narrow hall. I thought this was wonderful – I was fifty years too soon for 'smashing' or 'super'. Inside, to

89

the left, was the sunny sitting-room, comfortable, well lived-in and full of things, which my home didn't have – for instance, in the bay window were Venetian blinds which I was allowed to operate; there were more books than in all my other aunts'and uncles' houses put together; there was that well-used piano, with its yellowing ivories and its fretwork front backed by satin – at least, I think it was satin.

Outside the sitting-room door the steep, linoleum-covered stairs went straight up. Like the rest of the house they were spotlessly clean and smelt deliciously of furniture polish, but they were slippery. One day, I sat on the top stair to do up my shoelace, slipped, and went bumpety-bump all the way down, without any ill effects apart from fright. Upstairs, there were three bedrooms and a loo; there was no bathroom, although, later, one was carved out of the large front bedroom.

Downstairs, the narrow front hall did a double right-angled turn to avoid the staircase. On the left, behind the front room, was a smaller room, used only on special occasions. It was cool and darkish, lit only by a north window, which looked out on a small, shady courtyard, where we used to have tea on hot August afternoons. I used to like to go into this peaceful room and gaze at its contents, especially Aunt Clara's collection of heraldic china and a fine mahogany sideboard, which, looking back, I suspect must have been Regency or, more probably, very early Victorian – really the same thing, when one realises that Regency lingered on until Albert and the Great Exhibition polished it off. There was also a fascinating coloured print of General Bonaparte, with his troops in the backround – a fairly youthful Napoleon before he assumed his Imperial Crown.

The end of the passage led into the dining-room-kitchen, though its range was rarely used for cooking. This was another friendly room, with coconut matting on a lino floor, a dresser, a cupboard and a glass-fronted china cupboard, a table against the window, a windsor chair for Uncle Tom and smaller ones for the rest of us, a door into the courtyard and another into the scullery. The scullery was a lean-to, with a copper, a gas stove and a sink, and a little washing-up cubby-hole backing on to an outside loo. The gas stove fascinated me as a small boy; nobody else in our predominantly rustic family had one. I could scarcely believe it could engender heat comparable to our roaring inferno of a range at home – but there was nothing wrong with Aunt Clara's or Win's cooking or baking!

The back garden was narrow, probably no more than twenty feet wide, but it was fairly long, large enough for Uncle Tom to grow something of everything in the vegetable line; and on the opposite side of the garden path was a narrow border for flowers. At the far end, near the door into the next road, the gooseberry bushes screened the dustbin.

It is odd that such an ordinary house should arouse so much nostalgia. But was it ordinary? It was uncommonly well-designed for family living; it was stoutly built; it was tidy and friendly; it smelt nice, and it was inhabited by people who were very far from ordinary to a small boy.

It was a religious house. There were family prayers after breakfast on Sunday mornings – to all of them a natural and proper way of beginning a Sunday, but to me an ordeal to be endured. So very much of life and talk in the home centred in that other focal point in their life, Chapel; even the cricket I played and the rambles I went on with other boys were linked with New King Street Chapel. It must be well over thirty years since I last saw New King Street Chapel, and I have no clear mental picture of its exterior and, thus, of its date; probably it is Victorian. But, no matter: the ghost of John Wesley was there, and in many other places in Bath. The city was, indeed, one of his early and main centres of activity, and twelve miles away in Bristol is his New Room, the first Wesleyan Chapel. My cousins used to tell me stories of him which I have never since seen in print; maybe they were part of an oral tradition. Once, I was taken to the induction of a new minister. The greater part of the proceedings was taken up with an interminable, extempore prayer for all sorts and conditions of men, a home-made bidding prayer. This was punctuated with interjections by ancient crones and gaffers – 'Alleluia, God be praised!' or 'Amen, I say Amen to that', obvious survivals from the emotionalism of early Methodism.

The ordinary services at New King Street were conducted by the minister (or a lay preacher) in his large rostrum, with the choir, including Uncle Tom and the cousins, in a raked gallery behind him; I sat down below with Aunt Clara. I cannot remember much about these services. Some of the preachers ranted; one of them, when it came to the children's part of the service, would put on a nauseating grin, lean over the edge of the rostrum and talk down in both senses of the word – ugh! One minister, however, could preach better sermons than any I have suffered since – I actually listened to everything he said. He was well aware of his prowess! My cousins proudly informed me he was a New College man. I was suitably impressed, although he didn't look or sound particularly Oxford; later, I discovered there is a Methodist seminary of that name.

Aunt Clara must have sensed that Methodism did not fill me with joy and light. I don't think I made this too obvious, for I was a polite little prig. More likely it was an Edwards reaching out instinctively to an Edwards. Anyhow, she took me occasionally to Evensong at the Abbey, but I didn't care much for this either – everything was so remote, inaudible and well-nigh invisible, and those thousands of memorials plastered on the walls gave me the willies. It's no use – I was never geared to religion, least of all its revivalist forms. Besides, even then I knew that John Wesley was a near-apostate Anglican parson – not quite cricket! I remain an Anglican of sorts, even if an unbelieving and rarely practising one. Even today I jump to the defence of the Established Church when it is attacked; even today, I firmly believe that Dissenters (except Roman Catholics and Quakers) cannot possibly be gentlemen. Still, I don't suppose the Bishop of Bath and Wells will bother to excommunicate a nonentity who happens to regard Wells Cathedral as one of the loveliest buildings in the land.

My favourite vantage point in Bath was Beechen Cliff. There I could see nearly all the ancient heart of the City below me and rising up the opposite slopes to Lansdown. Cousin Win, patient and loving, answered all my questions. Even today, I think I could go back there and identify every church and main secular building. The Georgian city-planning didn't impress me, though, of course, I liked The Circus for its shape. Win told me about the Woods and Ralph Allen, but one has to be a dedicated Georgian or post-middle-aged to appreciate the lovely austerity of, say, Queen's Square. I was sold on churches, the more Gothic the better, and my favourite, most oddly, was St. John's, the building in South Parade. Pevsner rightly calls it 'rockfaced'. The Pisgah habit has stuck: when I visit an ancient town for the first time, I find a Beechen Cliff (or study a street plan) and fix my bearings by the parish churches.

Nobody ever had a better guide than Cousin Win, not even Dante–and he had Virgil! She took me everywhere: into Victoria Park with its collection of strange and stately trees, into peaceful Henrietta Park, into Sydney Gardens, on to the Recreation Ground, where incredibly ancient ladies in outmoded clothes played croquet with determination and guile. She fed my appetite for local quips and riddles–

'Why did Cedar Walk?'
'Because Oldfield Road'.
'When the lions on the entrance piers to Victoria Park hear the Abbey clock strike twelve, they toss the golden balls to one another.'

I still have this lust for verbal idiocies. We had morning coffee at Theobald's. This was an absolute 'must'– not only was the coffee excellent, but it was accompanied by a real Bath bun from Fortt's next door. Even today, at the first bite, I could tell, blindfold, the difference between a real Bath bun and a spurious one – that delicate flavour, those incomparable little baked lumps of sugar! Besides, what a name for a firm: Cater, Stoffel and Fortt; they sound like suppliers of tuckboxes to little Ruritanian princes.

We climbed – how we climbed! Up to the top of Little Solisbury, with its Iron Age fortifications; up to Brown's Folly; up to Lansdown, to the battlefield with its poignant memories of Sir Bevil Grenville, and to Beckford's tower, as nutty as the man himself; up to Ralph Allen's Sham Castle, a very satisfying Sham, though I didn't know then that it was probably designed by Sanderson Miller. We ventured well beyond the rim of the saucer which holds Georgian Bath – to Kelston Round Hill, to Englishcombe with its fascinating little church, to Limpley Stoke, then still remote and lovely. We often took that invigorating ride on the top of a tram to Coombe Down and back, and I always looked out for the old man actually sawing blocks of Bath stone in one of the quarries.

Aunt Clara, too, would occasionally take me around. Like her two sisters and three brothers (and one of her nephews!) she had a pre-auto cast of mind. Like them, she enjoyed being propelled around by an internal combustion engine, as long as someone else did the propelling. I doubt if anybody ever questioned her on the mechanism of a motor car, but if they had, I am quite certain her reply would include the family phrase that she "didn't know a bull from a bee's knee".

Just before the First Word War, and, again, immediately afterwards, the charabanc came into its own, and Aunt Clara would take me off for an afternoon trip. She was the first to bring me to that phenomenally attractive village of Castle Combe; she enabled me to see my first medieval castle of any significance, Farleigh Hungerford. How she loved the ride: she would sit bolt upright and would be dignified and gracious to fellow passengers who spoke to us. If the conversation around us became hilarious, or, in her words, 'too free', she would remain silent and try to look aloof and disapproving; but she never missed a word, and occasionally her lips would twitch. In those days each charabanc carried a courier. Some couriers knew their stuff; some didn't. Once, when passing near the south-west escarpment of the Cotswolds, our courier pointed to Nibley Knoll: "Ladies and gentlemen, you see that monument up there on that hill. That was put up to the memory of Tyndale, him what wrote the

New Testament." Aunt Clara forgot her dignity: she turned her face towards me and gave me a whopping great music-hall wink. She was an Edwards, bless her old heart!

Affection for that remarkable family compels me to add a postscript. Life at 30, Winchester Road went on steadily in the same old way; it seemed eternal, as Victoria's reign seemed in the 1890s. Then came the Second War and one of those Baedeker raids on Bath. The bombs came screaming down, and Aunt Clara cried, "We shall all be killed, we shall all be killed". Then the Edwards imp reasserted itself, and she laughed and grunted, "Hark at 'em, the dirty toads!" The roof had been off for a couple of hours, the windows and doors were all gone, and Aunt Clara, wrapped in blankets, was huddled with the others in their Morrison shelter. Then, but only then, she remembered her bronchitic tendencies and exclaimed, "Do you know, my dears, I think I feel a draught". Incidentally, in that wrecked house, not one single piece of her heraldic china was damaged.

The next morning my family brought them to Yatton. They stayed with my parents for a while, and then took a house in the village. On those rare occasions when I could get away from duties in a V.1. and V.2. area, I would go and see them, and note with delight at the salvaged reminders of boyhood, including General Bonaparte still waving on his troops to victory. Aunt Clara died at the end of 1946; Uncle Tom died in 1951, within a few days of his ninety-fourth birthday. The cousins, too, are now all gone. Win, the last, died at Christmas time, 1968, probably the day after she sent her Christmas card to me. I am glad I went to see her in the previous October. She had had a serious operation and was very frail. She reluctantly admitted she was far from well, and yet she hadn't altered greatly in appearance – there was still a good deal of the vibrant girl in the woman of seventy-six. It was like old times, and we talked happily about old times – it was a wonderfully eager, cheerful natter. Dear Win! I loved the whole family, but Win has a special niche in my affection.

Chapter Fifteen

UNCLE TED

Uncle Ted died in 1928, but, even now, over fifty years later, there are moments when I cannot believe it is true. Every so often he comes back in my dreams: I open a door and there he is, sitting massively on a small, hard chair, legs apart and hands on knees. I would say, "But I thought . . . ". He would puff at his cigarette and reply gently, "No, my little fellow, not quite; you musn't believe all you hear." The Freudians would probably have fun and games with this, but, to me, it is just a measure of my affection, for I loved him more than any other man.

He was one of the fat three – he, Aunt Louisa and Aunt Fanny; the other three, Uncle Willie, Aunt Clara and my father were stringy and took after the Yeates family, their mother's side. Uncle Ted was a true Edwards. He went bald early, and I knew him only when his remaining hairs were grey; but I was told he had been very fair in the Edwards way. He was broad and corpulent, with a bottom-heavy face like Henry VIII's, but his eyes were very different from Henry's – they were large, blue, heavily hooded and infinitely kind.

He was a kind father and an adorable uncle. He had six children of his own: his four boys were lively, but his mild rebukes were always effective. When one of them accidently walloped him over the head with a stick during a ratting foray, he rubbed the rapidly rising bump and murmured, "I shouldn't have done that if I had been you, my little fellow."

He always had *time* – time for children. "Don't go, yet, Uncle Edward; do come and play. It's not *late*." He would look around the company: "Well, what about it? Just half an hour, no more." The other grown-ups always agreed, and it was then up to my ingenuity to stretch that half an hour to an hour and a half. Sometimes it was dominoes, with a Double-Nine set of which I was tremendously proud; sometimes it was National Gallery with cards which dated from Grandmother Edwards' time. I wonder how many people remember those National Gallery cards, that Victorian combination of fun and education and my first experience of art history. Dad, Aunt Fanny, the cousins, all played with determination and guile. My mother was guileless, never won and delighted in other folk's cleverness. Uncle Ted just enjoyed himself. Sometimes he would pretend to cheat, especially if Aunt Fanny was really cheating. Sometimes he would give me a nudge and a conspirator's wink which meant, "I know *you've* got the Turner key card and *you* know your father has "Ulysses deriding Polyphemus" and "The Fighting Temeraire"; don't forget to skin him when your turn comes'. If he thought that I was being scalped too cruelly by

94

superstructure had lost most of the little comfort it had ever possessed. Uncle Ted and Owen were supposed to arrive in it at 5.30 a.m. to pick up my father. He stamped and raged outside the house for an hour and a half, and then the ancient chariot came chuffing along. Just as they were about to start off for Radnorshire, I noticed a pool of petrol under the car. Owen lifted the bonnet and found that the carburettor had nearly fallen off; he calmly tied it on tightly with a piece of string. Dad spluttered angrily, "What if the thing comes off again?" Uncle Ted replied equably, "Well, my little fellow, I expect Owen will tie it on again." The valiant car did the long double journey without incident and the trio returned jubilant in the early hours of the next day. About a week later, hundreds of scraggy little Welsh sheep arrived, and, with rather touching innocence, Dad ordered them to be turned into Gammer's Butts, usually known as Long Field. The following day, the field was empty: hedges presented no obstacle to sheep used to leaping from mountain to mountain in the wilds of Radnorshire. The round-up began, but quite a number were never found again; worse still, the gaff was blown – nobody would buy Edwards's wild little Welsh bastards! So Dad and Uncle Ted had to send them to their cousin Willy Edwards at the other end of the county with a plea to sell them off quickly and at any price before their wildness was discovered. The brothers broke about even, but never again went into Radnorshire.

Neither Uncle Ted nor my father ever drove a car or knew anything about the way it worked. Like myself, they enjoyed being driven around, but were just not interested in mechanical things. How they would have despised the modern cult of the car as a status symbol. To them, cars were new-fangled things which had their uses provided someone else did the fussing. *They* belonged to the horse age. Uncle Ted, for all his weight, rode superbly; both brothers drove with consummate skill. For fast driving, Uncle Ted favoured a dogcart; Dad preferred a gig. For jogging around, my uncle had a governess car, while we had that rarity, a Jubilee car, which was a governess car the other way round – you got in at the front. Uncle Ted thought highly of the Jubilee car and would always offer to drive it; besides, he was fond of Kitty, the pony, who drew it. I believe he had once owned her; she was sweeter-tempered than Spider, his own pony, who had a habit of biting your elbow when you weren't looking.

I cannot think of the Jubilee car without recalling Oliver Palmer, prince of roadmen, with his long brush with curved handle, the symbol of his office, his corduroy suit, his trousers tied below the knees with straps and his luxuriant Newgate fringe, rolling like an ocean wave from ear to ear and breaking on his shaven chin. He was working on his home beat near the Rhodyate, a steep and dangerous hill which in those days had a double bend at either base. The year must have been 1911 or 1912; anyhow, it was in the midst of one of those cycling crazes, when armies of cyclists would leave Bristol on Saturday afternoons to swoop on Cheddar or any neighbouring village for a strawberry-and-cream tea. Uncle Ted was driving my mother, Aunt Fanny and myself to Iwood Manor. As we were crossing the Congresbury base of the Rhodyate, a horde of cyclists came hurtling down the hill, those with fix-wheels resting their feet on the front forks of their machines. All of them, except one, spotted the Jubilee car in good time, swerved and flashed past us. The unfortunate one saw us too late wobbled, struck us amidships and landed in our laps. He was more frightened than hurt, but his bike was badly buckled. He started abusing my uncle, accusing him of being on the wrong side and threatening legal action. Uncle Ted puffed away at his cigarette and said gently, "Hush my poor little fellow, that is not so." Oliver Palmer saw the whole incident. For a moment or so, he rested his hands and chin on the handle of his broom; then he walked over with deliberation. "Good at'ernoon, Maister Edward, good at'ernoon ladies. Did I hear *he* zay you were on your wrong zide?" He then went to the cyclist's left hand side of the road, put each foot slowly in turn in front of the other and measured the distance. "Zeventeen of my veet, and I be zure they be more than a voot long. Volks like thee, my lad, ought to be zhut up." That settled it. All the same, Uncle Ted gave the cyclist five shillings and drove him to Congresbury village where his companions, who had missed him, were anxiously waiting.

Country folk in the West laugh more heartily and often than most English people. All my father's generation, except Aunt Clara, laughed prodigiously, without any inhibitions and sometimes in the wrong place. Aunt Clara was 'a bit proper', as we put it, but when some particularly ludicrous flea of a situation got under her corsets, she would beat the lot. Dad and Uncle Ted often laughed until the tears rolled down their cheeks and their breath almost gave out. But Uncle Ted also had his dead-pan side; Dad had it, too, but he couldn't keep it up for long. I was once in Uncle Ted's shop during his second spell as a butcher. A customer wanted some lamb chops, but none was handy, so Uncle Ted brought a fresh New Zealand carcass from the fridge. As he was unwrapping it, the woman noticed that the animal had been cut in two and the hindquarters impacted into the forequarters. "Mr. Edwards," she said, "What a funny shaped animal." "Yes, madam," said Uncle Ted solemnly, "in New Zealand they invariably grow like that; they are a very strange people, those Maoris." She believed him.

He rarely gave any clues to his inner, fundamental beliefs. He wasn't much of a churchgoer. In this matter, his generation of the Edwards tribe was evenly divided: he, Aunt Louie and Uncle William rarely saw much of their parsons; Aunt Clara, highly ethical, was a staunch Wesleyan and married to one; Aunt Fanny was an indomitable Anglican, and, though a spinster, managed somehow to be an active member of the Mothers' Union; Dad was one of the perpendicular pillars of the magnificent parish church – Vicar's Warden, C.E.M.S., Diocesan representative, the lot. But I firmly believe that my simple-natured, pious mother had more of the inner radiance of religion in her little finger than the six of them put together. They were incapable of *thinking* in a theological sense; they were not men and women of *faith*; they just *felt* about religion. Uncle Ted read the Bible a good deal on Sundays, and in moments of grief his spoken and written language had a strong biblical flavour. But this, like churchgoing, is no real evidence of religious depth.

I shall never be able to explain to others why I loved him so much. Perhaps it was because he was the quintessence of that generation of the family, especially in his finer qualities. His sense of fun was deeper even than his brothers' and sisters', There was nothing of the professional *nice* man about him – he didn't *seek* popularity or affection. He was not a *leader*; on the contrary, he was all for leaving people and things alone. Nor was he a father-confesssor type – he was far too diffident to invite or offer advice readily. It is just that people took one look at him, realised that here was a man of infinite, boundless kindness, gave him their affection without stint and received his in like measure.

Chapter Sixteen

THE REFUGE

Every human being needs a refuge, an ivory tower, a cell, a cave, a retreat, a place for contemplation, a place to be quiet in, above all, a place to be alone in. All through the ages, those with any whit of wisdom have realised this, from St. Anthony to Greta Garbo and Penelope Mortimer. Today, in this brittle, pinchbeck, cruel world of profitability, pop and paranoia, the need is even greater. Some are not aware of the need. Others are afraid to be alone – afraid to be confronted by their own emptiness. Of course it wouldn't do to be alone indefinitely: there is work to be done, and, anyhow, according to the slide-rule boys, the earth has to go on enduring for another five thousand million years before the day of final extinction. But everyone needs solitude – an opportunity to consider what he is and why he exists.

As a boy, my refuge was Cadbury; it still is on the rare occasions I can get there. It is a small hill, a mere two hundred and sixty-three feet at its highest point. It is the extreme spur at the tip of a plateau which spreads out northwards from the centre of the main Mendip ridge and then sinks westwards into the alluvial plain between Weston-Super-Mare and Clevedon. It has long been considered to be an Iron Age hill fort, but it was not as well-known as the Cadbury at Tickenham and nothing like as distinguished as South Cadbury, the so-called Camelot. Recently they have been finding interesting evidence there of Roman and post-Roman occupation. It has no startling beauty; to most of the few hundred people who know it, it is probably just a little hill; to me it is Patmos and Pisgah rolled into one.

Its top is about twelve hundred paces from my old home. The direct way leads up Henley Lane and past the cricket field where many years ago an Australian team played. The local club came back to it after the First World War (after the period which this book covers), and for forty years it was guarded, tended and loved by Frank Young. I played on it many a time in the 1920s, and in later years, whenever I returned home from exile, I could reckon on finding Frank there, summer or winter, on a Saturday afternoon. He was of near-county status, and had he been richer or poorer he would have played for Somerset, either as an amateur or as a pro. As it was, he must have headed the club batting or bowling averages, or quite often, both, for well over thirty years. A few springs ago, as I climbed over the stile opposite the entrance to the ground, I looked back half expecting to see him scratching the pitch or pouncing on an intrusive plantain. The field looked lovely in the pale, Irish-gold sunlight, but strangely empty.

Frank died in 1961; he was only fifty-seven.

The path from the stile rises gently, then more steeply, a red-clay streak in the green turf between bracken-covered slopes. Then it passes under a great oak, where many a time as a boy I would pick up, between finger and thumb, a greedy Red Admiral gorging itself on the sweet, sticky resin from a fungus near the base. Over fifty years later the spot was still excreting resin, though I haven't been there in Red Admiral time for many a day. Then the path moves upward again, now stony, past the grass-grown ditch and steep ramparts of the Iron Age fort, a place for courting couples who always seemed to find it quite convenient to make love at an angle of forty-five degrees. Then, on to the springy turf at the top, spattered with wild arums and tansy.

The top of the hill, the inner enclosure of the fort, is a long oval, perhaps three hundred and fifty yards by one hundred and thirty. The eastern half is full of grassgrown pits; the western half is pretty level. In the middle is a raised mound surmounted by the remains of a circular dry-stone wall enclosing a clump of trees. For over fifty years, I have known exactly what I would do if Cadbury were mine and I was a millionaire. I would level off that top and turn it into a cricket field. It would be singularly appropriate for that peculiarly English religion to be practised by its white-clad acolytes in an arena which saw strange rites more than two thousand years ago. Besides, the congregation, if a little bored, could turn around and look at the view.

I have always liked a nice view! Fifty years and more later, it is impossible for me to say exactly why the prospect from Cadbury was so fascinating to a small boy. This story is intended to be a truthful childhood autobiography; I would not consciously antedate any emotional experience and I will not expose myself to the danger of doing it unconsciously. Certainly I was aware of the pattern of colours and the depth of scenery which lay below and beyond me; certainly I took a delight in identifying and learning about every hill, church, house or field pointed out by any patient and knowledgable companion.

The best view has always been to the south. At the extreme left, half a mile away, are the wooded slopes of Kingswood, joined to Cadbury by the Rhodyate, now a straight up-and-down on the main Bristol – Weston road, but in my boyhood it was a steeper hill-road with a dangerous right-angled bottom corner at either end. Beyond Kingswood, four miles away across the Wrington Vale, the line of the Mendips begins and runs right across the vista from east to west. First comes Black Down, the highest point, the only sandstone in a limestone ridge, heather-covered and looking deep blood-red in the distance. Chiselled into the limestone covering its flanks is Burrington Combe, with its Rock of Ages, where the Reverend Augustus Toplady sheltered from the storm and thought up the hymn. To a small boy it was my favourite hymn next to Onward Christian Soldiers. I wonder why – it couldn't be the banal words of that rigid Calvinist; it must have been the pseudo-dramatic tune.

In front of Black Down, at a lower level, are Mendip Lodge Wood and Dolbury. They have pulled down Mendip Lodge, with its memories of Mrs. Henry Wood, but as a boy with exceptionally good eyesight, I could stand on Cadbury and pick out its Italianate form and long verandah. I didn't care much for *East Lynne*, but, oddly enough, *Mrs. Haliburton's Troubles* used to thrill me to the marrow. Dolbury has always overawed me. I see that Pevsner calls it 'a vast and splendid Iron Age Earthwork, one of the largest and most impressive monuments of its class in Great Britain'. As a boy, I found it a solitary and melancholy place; I didn't know then that it was a fortress, a refuge – I thought a camp was a permanent dwelling place and wondered how people could continue to exist in that stony and windswept enclosure.

Westwards the Mendips split into two more or less parallel lines. In front are the wooded slopes of Sandford Hill, Banwell Camp and Banwell Hill; behind them at a higher level are Wavering Down and Crooks Peak. Between, and visible from Cadbury only with the inward eye, is Yarborough where great-great-grandfather, Joseph Edwards, appeared from oblivion in 1781 as a comfortable farmer in the valley of the Lox Yeo. He died in 1835, aged eighty-eight, and then, probably a year later, at least two of his sons left Yarborough and went to Nempnett Thrubwell where my grandmother, Deborah Yeates, was living, a little girl of seven. I didn't discover these family dates until about twelve years ago, but I knew about old Joseph and Yarborough when I was a small boy. This is an example of how the past is preserved in the countryside. My father was born in 1872, but he remembered accurately the family stories he was told by his mother (born 1829) which she had heard when she was a girl. I have checked everything he told me against parish registers and other evidence. He was uncannily accurate; only in one small instance did he place a distant kinsman in the wrong generation. Incidentally, I am passing on what I have gleaned to my nephew, Bill, who has a lively young son, Arthur. Who said that family solidarity is breaking down nowadays?

Westwards still, the Mendips, now a single line again, rise through Bleadon Hill and then sink into the Severn at Brean Down, though the Steep Holm, in the Channel, is a lone outlier. And all along their journey to the sea, just under their skyline to the south and hidden from Cadbury, runs an ancient road. Today, it is sometimes a stretch of main road, sometimes a by-road, sometimes a track or footpath, sometimes lost altogether. When I was a boy, old Mansey, the schoolmaster, told me that it was the way by which the last Roman legions from Salisbury left this land. I have never seen any proof of this, but it is a nice touch and deserves to be true.

Truth is a tricky bucket to draw up from the well of memory. I cannot recall in detail all my boyhood reactions to the Wrington Vale and the alluvial plain, that depth of scenery between Cadbury and the Mendips. Take, for instance, the village of Congresbury and its church. I had virtually no knowledge of church architecture, but I liked that elegant tower and spire pushing upwards from the surrounding elms. I knew it had the finest ring of bells in a Vale noted for good peals; I knew the tenor was thirty-eight cwts. and I knew exactly how the bells were hung in the tower. I was aware of the fierce rivalry between Congresbury and our own village: we could easily wallop them in the Cheddar Valley League matches, but they were renowned as vigorous cup fighters, too vigorous for our lads, the Lily Whites. Then there was always the fun of identifing the homes of friends and kinsmen. I would vainly screw up my eyes to pick out Pineapple Farm, Uncle Willie's home, on the far side of Congresbury village. Old Mrs. Hardwick's cottage, however, was clearly visible no more than half a mile away. She was Uncle Ted's mother-in-law, a tough old girl, with a sharp tongue and a warm heart. When she was well into her seventies she would still dig and plant her garden – and stick up for herself when an unkind neighbour built a lean-to shed against her garden wall. The rainwater from the shed poured down her garden path and into her cottage. She protested; he was rude; she picked up her spade and cried, "I'll settle him". Then she dug a trench against the wall so that the water soaked back into his shed. But I remember her best as the finest creator of homemade wines; her plum wine, over forty years old, was as smooth as silk and as subtle as a serpent.

When I was about twelve, I began to visit Cadbury for its sunsets. Old Mansey, the schoolmaster, put me up to this; he said that the sunsets across the Bristol Channel were the best he had seen since those fantastic sunsets of his own boyhood, when Krakatoa blew its head off in 1883 and sent a layer of volcanic dust around the world. I learnt later that Tennyson, staying with the Eltons at Clevedon, used to look across the Channel to those sunsets behind the Welsh hills, those burning reds, those deep purple stratus clouds, and, higher up, the pale violets and translucent greens. I also learned, years later, that their prosaic cause was similar to that which Krakatoa engendered – all those particles of dust rising from industrial South Wales.

There were times when I did not bother to look outwards from Cadbury. There were so many fascinating corners and patches to be visited on the top of the hill itself and on the slopes: the secret path down through the bushes to the Coppice, a small house long owned by Uncle Ted and occupied by him during a short period of financial stringency; the spot where enormous and heavily fragrant white violets grew, and still grow; a vein in the rocks where the felspar crystals were specially variegated; the perfect slide down smooth rocks with that bump in the middle which sent you up in the air. At the top, near the west end – the Channel view – lay my favourite seat. How angry I used to get if I found somebody else sitting on it. It was a flat slab of limestone about a foot high with another wide stone, at grass level, as a footstool. In the lower stone was a hole, often containing spent wax vestas. I was determined when I grew up that I would sit on my stone, light my own cigarettes and throw my own wax vestas into that natural ashtray. Alas, by the time I got round to smoking, wax vestas has disappeared from the market. Near this stone, on a glorious Sunday summer afternoon in 1912 or 1913, I saw soldiers in khaki for the first time – a platoon of Royal Engineers on heliograph practice. I longed to be close to them, but was afraid if I left my seat that someone would dare to sit on it. Curiosity won: I stood enthralled as they watched and read aloud the winking light from Bleadon Hill far across the Vale – Y-O-U-R L-I-G-H-T I-S R-O-T-T-E-N. I was thrilled by the Officers' Sam Brownes and shining brown boots and by the uninhibited language of the N.C.Os; there were quite a number of words new to me. I didn't know the Morse Code, but I went home and 'pretended', using my father's shaving mirror until he stopped me pretty sharply. He was fussy about it, as indeed he was about all his immediately personal possessions; he rarely used it for shaving, but regularly when brushing his hair and twirling the ends of his moustache.

But, above all else, Cadbury to me was a paradise for butterflies. It was Hugh Mansey, the schoolmaster, who started me off on butterfly study; and by great good luck there was a copy of W. J. Lucas's manual in the pile of books on the sitting room sideboard. I was also encouraged by Jack Crease, 'Uncle' Jack Crease's son. Jack, a young officer in the Somerset Light Infantry, had been invalided out with a severe head wound in 1917. During his convalescence he took up, first, embroidery, and then, butterfly collecting, and he would often lend me his copy of South, one of the best books Warne's ever published.

Throughout the late summer of 1917 and the whole summer of 1918 I haunted the place. There was hardly a fine Saturday or August weekday when I was absent. Occasionally I would go over to Kingswood and Goblin Combe or down to the marshland meadows, but even then my heart was on Cadbury. I came to know the right places and the right times. There were two widely separated spots, one about twenty yards north of my stone seat, the other against Henley Wood, a spur of Cadbury. Here, in both places, high around the tops of the ash trees were the Purple Hairstreaks; here I would wait for ages for one of them to come down to the lower branches, within reach of my net. There was another spot just below the middle top of Cadbury, where a Green Hairstreak could occasionally be seen. Below it, along the south slope, was a footpath between brambles; this was my morning beat for about an hour or so. Near one of the Purple Hairstreak haunts, on the fringe of Henley Wood, was a bracken covered patch, good for Fritillaries – Pearl Bordered early on, and Dark Green and an occasional Silver Washed in high summer. In the glades of Henley Wood itself there were a few, a very few, White Lettered Hairstreaks.

The best place of all was a high, right-angled bank just under the north side of Cadbury and Henley Wood. Here I could follow the sun around: I would stay on the east slope during the late morning, after I had come away from the south side of Cadbury itself; then, in the afternoon, I would prowl around the south slope. The bank was covered with close turf, small bramble bushes, wild thyme and Tom Thumbs; on the flat ground below were nettles and clover. It was ideal: I could expect to meet almost anything in due season – Orange Tips and Brimstones: Wood Ringlets, straying from the glades of Henley Wood; Holly Blues around the ash trees at the top of the bank; Common Blues, Brown Arguses, Small Coppers and two or three kinds of Skippers on the slopes and flat ground; plenty of Peacocks and small Tortoiseshells; occasional Commas, Red Admirals and Painted Ladies; Browns of various kinds; and twice, but only twice, a Clouded Yellow. It was on this bank that I learned patience, something which never comes naturally to an Edwards, for we are all a hasty, impetuous lot. I learned to stand still, wait and watch for a butterfly to pitch and then walk slowly towards it, with the sun in front of me; and if the butterfly would not pitch, then the thing to do was to wait for it to return, which it often did.

Those butterflies of Cadbury gave me sunny hours of contentment. But the hill has been a retreat at all hours of the day and night and all seasons of the year. I have climbed it on moonlit nights and when it was deep with winter snow. I have stood on the top during a ferocious storm, with lightning illuminating the black edge of the Mendips. I went there to see the huge bonfire burning to celebrate the Coronation of George V and to another one shortly after the Armistice of 1918. I was frequently there with my fellow scouts – it was an ideal place for tracking and ambushing, and, indeed, for lighting fires, which, as everybody knows, are produced by rubbing two Boy Scouts together. I have been there when miserable and sick of the sight of human beings, and have always come away feeling a little less *pianissimo*.

How much longer I shall be able to visit it, I cannot say. There is not much time left, perhaps a very few years at the most. It is decrepitude I fear more than death – I would be infuriated if prevented by physical incapacity from making the climb. When I do pack up, I would prefer my body to be burned as there would then be just about enough ash and bone meal to keep a rose-bush going for a season. But I have no yearning for immortality; that is a foolish vanity. Besides, there isn't such a thing – the five thousand million years of this world's future are a mere drop in the ocean of eternity. But if anybody felt obliged to erect a memorial to me, I would rather it were on the top of Cadbury, up there with the Old 'uns, than down in the churchyard with those who held a faith I cannot share. Perhaps it is a primitive desire to be remembered transiently in that solitary place which was my boyhood refuge and consolation; the place to which I often return on the wings of troubled thought, to which I lift up mine eyes – though where the help comes from, Lord alone knows.